ENLIGHTENED

A Novel

Ericka Reynolds

A special thank you to Michelle Rosenfarb, writer of the movie "Bruised". Your understanding of how/why we find ourselves in the alternative healing/mindfulness world is precisely why I am now living my soul's purpose as a healer!
"No one decides to become all Zen and practice meditation and all that 'cause they did everything right." Bobbi "Buddhakan" Berroa (Sheila Atim)
Thank you Sheila Atim for representing the many women of color in the alternative healing/mindfulness world!

Dedication

Don't let the black woman in chains fool you.

This book is dedicated to those who want desperately to follow their dreams, but are still holding themselves back.

Yes, I am a black woman—an African-American woman, to be exact or politically correct—but this mindset goes beyond the image on the cover. I hope this story will touch everyone who has imprisoned herself or himself in something they know is not right, be it their job, their romantic relationship, their relationship with God, with their friends, their children—or with themselves.

"No one decides to become all Zen and practice
meditation and all that 'cause they did everything right."

— B O B B I " B U D D H A K A N " B E R R O A
(S H E I L A A T I M)

From the movie "Bruised".

A Special Note from the Author

My soul's purpose is to support you!

While Ava is a fictional character, she is nearly 100% me and experiences events that have taken place in my life.

Book 2, "Enlightened", dives into Ava's exploration of alternative healing where she finds the support she's been longing for to make much needed changes in her life.

Ava's experiences in Book 2 are what led me to become an Intuitive Life Coach. I am now able to support others in their healing journeys as a Certified Reiki Master Teach, Chopra Ayurveda Perfect Health Teacher, Spiritual Counselor, Sound Healer and Mindfulness Life Coach.

It brings me great pleasure to see how far I've come from the darkest places to being a healer and a source of light and love for others! My clients are thriving as they reconnect with their souls and begin living out their soul's propose!

If you should discover while reading this book that you are yearning to awaken your soul, reconnect with your soul or are

seeking to obtain the courage to move out on your soul's
mission feel free to connect with me!

The services and workshops I offer are listed at the back of this
book.

Thank you and happy reading!

ENLIGHTENED

A Novel

Prologue

I'm about to look up the National Park Service's Underground Railroad sites, only it's 1 AM and I am exhausted, so I pause my search and decide tomorrow, or more accurately, later today would be a better time for this activity. As I turn off my laptop and get ready for bed, I begin to think about my current enslavement.

Some would and some have told me I am crazy for wanting to leave my life at the Pentagon (aka Shawshank). It's a good job, it pays well, and I have these wonderful benefits. Why am I so hell bent on escaping from something that allows me to live such a wonderful life? Why would I leave to go off and pursue my writing thing full time?

I wonder how many slaves didn't make any of those trips with Harriet because someone got in their ear and subsequently in their head about how crazy it was to leave the plantation. How many slaves thought it was best, or safe, to stay put? Why risk the unknown when the known wasn't all that bad? They had a place to sleep, food to eat – isn't that enough? Should they want more than the basics out of life? Why should they want to travel to an unfamiliar place, start a new life with nothing? Nothing but their pride and their sense of freedom, that is.

I don't suppose my situation is much different. I am always on the defensive whenever I tell my family I am ready for a change. They don't get it. To them, the Pentagon is the motherlode! They were born and raised in the deepest part of the segregated South in the '50s and '60s. They picked cotton in the sweltering Southern heat. I am a fool to walk away from this good money and good benefits. Who in the hell do I think I am to believe I can make it on my own without the aid of the system?

Yep, there were many slaves that said fuck this shit and followed Harriet, and there were many others who were scared as shit to leave. Maybe not at first but after allowing some scared soul to infiltrate their mind, they stayed put and died on that damn plantation.

They stayed, they got beat down, they died.

If I stay, I too will continue to get beat down only my beatdown is in the form of blatant racism, favoritism and nepotism resulting in not getting another promotion and my death will come at the ripe old age of 57 – the earliest I can receive my freedom papers (retirement).

For me, the answer is escape to the unknown. There is not another option.

1

What Lies Ahead

Although I had lived in that house for five years, there's no emotional downside to leaving. The property owner was quite an ass right before I moved out, suddenly wanting to fix things that I had complained about for years. Now, he needed to get them done the week before I headed out of town. He had contractors knocking on my door at the crack of dawn and had the nerve to tell me I couldn't leave the house until the handyman repaired the backdoor and the paint dried. Of course, I kicked the dude out after his first coat of paint. It was the day of my going away party and I had to drive all the way to Waldorf, MD. Oh, well.

He's such an ass, *and* a Republican. He has a bumper sticker that says, "Fire Obama." I can't believe I gave this man rent for five years. I did reply to his last email, though, and made a note of my distaste for his behavior. His wife wrote back apologizing, and told me they enjoyed me as a tenant, not to worry about any more repairs, and to have a safe trip. I don't speak up for myself often enough, so sending that email sure felt good.

In any case, we're leaving now. The dogs are in the car and I've quadruple-checked everything. I'm dropping the keys into the mail slot back through the door.

This shit is over.

We're heading down South for a couple of days to see my family and then on to California. I am ready for this new chapter of my life, but I'm a little sad. After Dan stopped by yesterday to say his goodbyes, I don't know what I'm feeling other than completely unsure of what the year will bring for us. I'll be back next month for the fellowship orientation. I just hope he'll want to see me since we are taking a friends-with-benefits hiatus for the next year.

Perhaps I should just let it go now and start anew. Perhaps I should be completely free, with my heart wide open, so that when I meet Shemar Moore there will be no hang-ups (a fantasy, yes, but I am heading to the L.A. area for a year, so why not dream). I love the thought of meeting Shemar while I'm out there, and of us falling madly in love with each other. It could happen, as celebrities do sometimes date regular people. I could retire my vibrator for good!

More realistically, I can't believe I'm leaving town without telling Monique that this LR-7 device is not working. I've been Zenning in right-brain mode, so to hell with it, I'm going to California this way. Plus, it's a fellowship, not a real job. Now I'm playing devil's advocate. I have this device in my head and the controller in my arm. Maybe I should've gotten it fixed with a tune-up or something before leaving the area. Instead, I just got my hair done and lied about it operating correctly. I don't know . . . maybe I'll make time to see Monique while I'm back for the orientation next month . . . or maybe I won't. But I like keeping my secret. I like being in control of this part my life even though it's the one thing I should be scared shitless about. Who in the hell let's their hairdresser/former engineer operate on their brain and implant a device in it – a device that stopped working some time ago and for all I know is slowly melting my brain? But at least it got stuck in right brain mode. I am so sure I would have been running, crying, and begging for Monique to fix it had it gotten stuck in left brain mode.

"Alright girls! Say good-bye to our house! We love you house even though you are owned by a racist asshole! Thank you for the many years of shelter and comfort!"

I pull off from the house and head down the street with the music blasting. It's going to be a long and yet short eight hours to get to Columbia South Carolina. Long drive yes and short because once we pull up in the driveway of my parents' house, we are going to wish we still had hours left to go.

Spending time with my family is a miserable experience. I visit out of some twisted sense of obligation, only be to made fun of and told how fat I am. I really think my parents are missing a few screws, or perhaps they just don't love me, and they are quite aware of their mistreatment of me. This hazing (for lack of a better word) has been going on ever since I can remember. I walk by, and my mom will pull at my hair and ask things like, "Why did you cut your hair? Or dye it, or style it that way?" They both love to tell me how grossly overweight I am, though I am not at all on the brink of obesity. I used to give my mom my old clothes, not because they were too small, but just because my style had changed. Every time, she would hold them up, look them over and say, "Wow they are so huge! I'll have to take them in a lot to wear them." A simple thank you would have sufficed. And, considering they were all size twos, I would always question if she were mentally okay or somewhat delusional. So, I just stopped giving her my clothes. And now that I am a size four, forget it. Not giving her my clothes seemed simple enough until she asked me why I stopped bringing her things. When I told her I didn't need to be told I was fat in exchange for doing something nice for her, she just looked at me and said, "But you are." I wanted to scream, "A size two is not fat, damn it!" Instead, I just walked out of the room. My dad is no better. He likes to stand right next to me, lean over and whisper, "You are getting those hips, just like your aunts! Does it bother you when you walk with all that extra weight?" I never respond. I simple walk away. I have to believe they can see I am not fat... I know one thing: I can see they are crazy as shit.

The fat remarks are only a small part of the torturous visits, but for the twenty years since I've graduated college, I make a point to spend time with them. This time, I went out of my way to make the trip since South Carolina is not enroute to California.

As predicted, the eight hours have gone by extremely fast, and we are here in the driveway. I am sitting in my shiny new certified pre-owned Range Rover Evoque with the car still running. I know they know we are here. I know this because I just spoke to them not even thirty minutes ago when they called to asked how far out I was. I know they know I am here because my mother is constantly peeking out of the windows. And yet no one comes out to greet us. Never have and never will. I open the door and move to get the girls out of their car seats. They are excited to be here. Not because they enjoy my parents but happy to be getting out of the car. I always stop two, sometimes three times on the way down to let them stretch their little legs and get a treat. I also am sure these stops are for me to prolong this experience but alas it only buys me about thirty or forty-five extra minutes.

"Okay sweet babies! Let do this!"

As I reach to unbuckle Sophie, my yorkie, who always sits on the left side of the car, I feel my heart beginning to race. It always does so it's not surprising just I would think after years of this it would be old hat at this point. I pick Sophie up and move around to the passenger side of the car to get Cleo, my poodle. She is jumping up and down and shaking her little body with delight. With both dogs out I walk with them to the front door. I have a key that my mom gave me a few years ago so I use it to open the door.

As we enter, I see my dad on the couch reading the paper and my mom in the kitchen washing dishes. Neither glance our way but my dad manages to say, "Hey Cleo and Sophie! You came to visit your granddaddy!" I drop their leashes and let them run over to say hello. Their excitement to be near him will fade within the hour but it is cute to see especially if I pretend in this moment that I belong to a somewhat normal functioning family. I turn to go back to the car to grab a few things – the girls' food, toys, beds, treats, water, and a duffle bag for me. As I reenter the house, I see my mom is coming back inside the kitchen from the backyard with the girls. "I let them out to potty cause I know they haven't been all day."

"We just stopped at the South Carolina Welcome center (approximately 1 hour and 45 minutes ago)."

"That's what I said, they haven't peed all day."

"Right."

"We don't have anything to eat but there is some soup that I froze last week. I can thaw that out for you."

"No thank you I ate on the way down."

"Um yeah I sure you did. Some junk food, right?"

"Not many choices along I-95."

"They sell salads at those places to you know."

"I checked with the girls and neither Cleo nor Sophie felt like driving so I could eat a salad so opted for a grilled chicken sandwich."

"That is still full of grease and fat and that's why you have all those hips on you."

"Of course, it is."

"Your sister said you can come over and see her tonight."

"Thanks, but I think we are going to do that tomorrow. I just want to go to bed."

"You would have time today if you would leave early. I don't know why you can't get up at four or five in the morning like we do when we travel."

Pure procrastination in getting here but I will keep this thought to myself. And no thank you Ava for going out of your way to see us on your way to California. Just you're fat and make poor fast-food choices. Yep, different visit, same thing.

"You can call her and tell her you're not coming."

"I certainly can but I just told her that about an hour ago when she called to asked me where I was."

"Oh, well she just called right before you got here and told me to tell you to come over."

My family has some serious control issues.

I grab the girls' bag and head into the kitchen to feed them dinner. My mother follows. Their kitchen is nondescript. White cabinets, white appliances, white kitchen table with white chairs.

There it is, the yank of my hair. "What's this?"

"Weave."

"Why do you need weave? You done went and messed up your hair again?"

I stop and take a breath and look fully at my mother. She is a short lady. Shorter than me – maybe 4'11". She weighs 90 pounds and looks malnourished but she is proud of herself for looking this way. Her black hair which she is pulled back into a ponytail is showing more gray streaks and you can see pure exhaustion on her pecan-colored face.

"I didn't mess up my hair. I used to wear weaves all the time and then I stopped and now I've decided to start back. It's called having choices."

"It looks ridiculous"

Ignoring her I pull out the girls' food, bowls, and water. I pour a bowl of water and set it on the floor and then get their food ready. As I put their bowls down my dad enters the kitchen.

"I made some ham hocks and collard greens. You want some? I heard your momma say we didn't have anything to eat but that's because I made these and she didn't, so she doesn't think they're good."

"She don't want that."

"How do you know?"

"Cause she don't eat stuff like that, do you?"

"Actually, yes I do, and you know this. Why…never mind." "No, I am full but thank you."

"There's plenty so you can have some tomorrow. Maybe your mom will be nice and make us some cornbread to go with it."

"Ava knows how to make cornbread if y'all want some and you don't need to be eating that mess anyway. Too much salt and fat."

My mom leaves the kitchen to go watch television. I am left in the even more uncomfortable company of my father as I watch Cleo and Sophie finish their dinner and find their way to my mom in the living room. I can't imagine they enjoy her company that much but there is such a heavy feeling around my dad that I think they prefer to hang out with my mom.

I bend over to grab their bowls and head to the sink.

As I start to wash them, he speaks.

"So, you ready for this long trip out to California?"

"Yep."

"Man, this is crazy huh?"

"What's crazy?"

"You getting selected to go out there. I mean there are thousands of people they could have selected, and they picked you huh?"

"Yep, they did."

"Did they say why?"

"Because I am qualified."

"Hum."

It's the hum that makes me take a long look at him too. He stands about 5'7" and has a receding hairline and a bald spot in the middle of his head but little gray. His walnut-colored completion still looks quite youthful, older but not as worn down as my mother.

"Well, whatever the reason, they picked me, and I am going."

"That's all you can do."

What does that even mean in this context? I don't even think I care to know. I dry the bowls and walk past my dad. As I leave the kitchen, I tell Cleo and Sophie I am heading to bed, and we need to take one more potty break. The girls who are curled up on my mom's lap hop up and follow me through the dining room into the kitchen and out the back door. It's just a few days Ava and you did this to yourself. You decided to come here first. Why I don't know but I will say while their insults are the same, they seem to be rolling off me easier. I wonder if that's the right brain mode at work or if after all these years I am finally numb to the crazy.

As we head back in, we say good night to my mother. My dad has made his way to their bedroom so that is one less good night to give.

I pick up my bag that I left at the door and head to the bedroom. I pull out my pajamas and head back out to the bathroom. I do love that there is a door that closes off the bedrooms and bathrooms so once I am back here I am mostly alone though I can set my watch by it my mom will make her way back here as soon as she thinks I am out of the bathroom. She will appear, check on us, make sure we are okay and behave like a loving concerned mother. This appearance will last for only the moments when she is alone with me and the girls in the bedroom. Sometimes I think she feels she must play along with the we hate Ava thing for my dad but if so, damn she deserves an Oscar! I am sure I could have unpacked this during the many therapy sessions I've had but I think I choose to live with the mystery to further torture myself.

"Hey! Just checking to see if you need anything?"

"Nope, we're good."

She is now making up the second twin bed for Cleo and Sophie. She has their beds along with pillows and throws. It always looks so cozy. They hop up on the bed and curl up though I know they will find their way to my bed as soon as she leaves. Sleeping with two dogs on a twin bed is rough even though they are super tiny it still makes for an awkward sleeping arrangement.

"Okay, I'll see you all in the morning. I'll make you some pancakes and sausage. Did you call your sister?"

"No. She will be alright."

"That she will. Goodnight. See y'all in the morning."

"Goodnight and thank you for the pancakes."

She closes the door and I plug my phone into the charger. I as I do I see there are no missed calls, no text messages. Maybe I should send Dan a text? Maybe not. Maybe I should let him miss me. Maybe he won't. I decide to turn off the light and crawl under the covers. Cleo and Sophie join me on my bed, and we cuddle up for the night.

Somehow I am not having pancakes at home with my mom, but I am dressed up and heading to breakfast with my dad. He wants me to meet some friends of his at this place across town. The drive is quite and all I know is that he told them he would bring me by. I am not sure how you can promise people that your grown daughter is going to do something, but I am in this car, in a dress, cute wedges and fully made up at 10 AM. Being somewhat militant about this meeting I elected to wear all beige. Beige crochet dress with a beige slip underneath hitting just at the knee, beige wedges, weave down with a few curls I added this morning. I don't want to be here in this car going to meet some of his old Army buddies. I know this is another show off moment.

As we arrive and enter the restaurant, I am surprised to see my dad wave at his buddies and then ask the hostess to seat us. I thought surely we were here to spend time with them.

"I know what you're thinking. Why not join them?"

"That was my thought, yes."

"They are too much, and I wanted us to have some alone time."

This is strange as we don't do alone time. I glance over at table and see the same look of confusion on about ten faces. These men surely thought we were joining them for breakfast but now my dad has separated us from them. We order our food and I wait for the fat joke, but it doesn't come. Our breakfast is served, and we eat in silence. After our meal, the crew is still there, loud and enjoying themselves.

"Let's go over and I will introduce you."

We get up and head to the other side of the restaurant. As we approach the table my dad does that thing he does. "Hey fellas! I want to introduce you to my youngest baby girl, Ava. Ava, these are the men I spent my Army career with."

They all yell out their hellos and I smile, and say, "It's nice to meet you all." One gentleman speaks and says, "Ms. Ava! Your daddy can't stop bragging about you! Man, all we ever hear about is you! He is so proud of you! Ms. Pentagon! And now heading out to California! You were handpicked to go out of thousands he said. Congratulations!"

Ain't this some shit? Just last night he seemed confused as to why I was selected but apparently he has been bragging to all of his buddies about this fellowship. Hum, some kind of shit.

"Thank you!"

The rest of the conversation is a blur as I watch my dad make his way around the table slapping them on their backs and cracking jokes. When he has completed his performance he makes his way back to me, puts his hand on my shoulder and says, "Gentlemen we've got to head out now, but I will be here next month for our breakfast meeting!"

"See you man!"

"Have a good day!"

"Nice meeting you Ava!"

"You done good man!"

And more goodbyes echo as we walk away.

I turn back to look at them. All are seemingly happy for my dad, for his success which is me. I think this is like having a slave stand on an auction block while someone points out their attributes only I didn't get sold to the highest bidder, I just got ushered back to the same plantation. I wonder how they would feel if they knew my success was despite him and not because of him. They would probably still count it as his victory.

I am so thankful to be back at their house a feeling I don't think I've ever had before. Spending time alone with my dad has always been so extremely uncomfortable for me. I never know how things are going to go but without fail there is always a good insult or two and today nothing. Other than that auction block moment.

As I get out the car my dad heads towards to mailbox and then begins speaking with a neighbor across the street. I open the door and I am greeted with love! There they are! My girls run up to me to say hello and follow me to the kitchen. My mom rounds the corner from the hallway and enters the kitchen. "There's coffee if you want some."

"Do you have any cream?"

"No."

"Then no."

"We have sugar."

"Yes, but I like cream and sugar."

"That's what you say but you can drink it without cream."

"I could but I don't like it that way."

"I thought about buying some when I was at the store the other day since you were coming but I didn't get any."

"I should have stopped on the way here and I didn't. I'll go out later and get some."

"That's a waste of money. Especially when you can drink it without cream."

"Do you have any milk?"

"No, you know we don't drink milk anymore."

"Right."

This is the same conversation we have every time I am here. I feel like it's an exceedingly small thing to do, have cream for you daughter who is coming to town but nope, never the case. Of course, whenever they visit me, I have all their favorites and they would be appalled if I didn't but this thought is petty so I will let it go and go to the store later plus we will need milk to make the cornbread for dinner.

Facebook, July 4, 2015
As we celebrate Independence Day, I can't help but be reminded of all the wonderful things that I was able to experience in and around our nation's capital. These are just a few of those remarkable things that were still saved on my phone 😊

Posting on Facebook is fun though I can't see how some of my family and friends find the time to post several times a day. I simply plan to use it to keep everyone updated on my cross-country trip. It will be better than when I drove from Oklahoma to Virginia in 2007. I spent most of each evening making phone calls to let folks know I had made it to my next stop safely. And, of course each call was thirty minutes or more which meant I got little sleep before waking up, walking the girls, feeding them, repacking the car, and heading on to the next stop. Thank you, Facebook, for a quick post. Though this has nothing to do with my trip to California, I feel a sense of obligation to share as I scroll through other people's Fourth of July posts. I really don't see how people can be on this thing all the time.

And now over to my sister's house. I have managed to only spend an hour or so with her since I arrived the other day and that was plenty of time for me. My sister and I are complete opposites. Not one thing in common so it makes for an exceptionally boring time together. Not strange and awkward like with my dad though she can certainly hit below the belt as well. I don't blame her though as she's only doing what she's learned from them. She's seen them treat me like crap all her life so it would be impossible for her to think to treat me any other way.

As I drive down the street to her house, I blast the radio. My favorite R&B station in this city still plays the best songs! I remember growing up here and listening to this station. Ah the 80s! The Michael Jackson, Tina Marie, Prince days! Of course, these were also the Madonna, Culture Club and Cyndi Lauper days but something about Soul music and Soul Train in the 80s just brings back good memories. I was living with these same crazy people, but the music and that show was a great escape for me.

I am now parked in my sister's driveway. Just sitting here. I always use the excuse of needing to get back to my parents' house to feed the girls and so I time my visits about an hour or two before dinner allowing my escape from her home to seem necessary. Of course, it's an escape from one not so great place to another not so great place. I should be questioning why I come down here so often especially this trip that has absolutely nothing to do with driving West. Sure, you can get to California from here, but you most certainly can leave Virginia and find your way to the West Coast without ever getting on I-95 South.

I finally open the door and walk up the steps to the front porch. I ring the bell and wait and wait. Finally, she appears and opens the door. "Hey! I thought you would have been here by now."

"I just called you and told you I was leaving mom and dad's and it's only a five-minute drive so I am not sure how much sooner I could have been here." Why am I explaining this to her?

"I guess. I thought you called a while ago."

"Oh."

"Come in!"

I follow her inside and look around. I am amazed she lives in this big house by herself, but the cost of homes is inexpensive down here so why not I guess. As she makes her way to the family room I follow slowly thinking about the nice big house I sold in Oklahoma. Maybe I should have stayed but it would have only been for the house, so I guess that's an insane reason. I do miss my screened in porch and gazebo daybed swing in the backyard. Maybe running away from heartbreak was a mistake. I certainly didn't find love on the East Coast just an asshole with commitment issues. At least in Oklahoma I had a nice home to relax in and the predictability of tornado season.

"Ava!"

"Huh?"

"I asked if you wanted something to drink, eat?"

"A soda would be good, thanks."

I am now standing in the family room watching her stand in front of the open refrigerator. My sister is about 5' 5" and has beautiful milk chocolate brown complexion. She's got the height, gorgeously long thick jet-black hair, and shapely body that I wish I had also obtained from our parents' DNA. She reaches in and hands me a can of ginger ale. I move towards her to get it and smile.

"Thanks."

"Sure, so how's your visit going since I've only seen you a second?"

"Not bad, went to breakfast with dad the other day"

"Yeah, he said he was going to take you to meet his friends. You know we are all proud of you even though it's crazy of you to move out to California for a year."

"Why would you say that?"

"Because that is a lot of work for a short time. Giving up your rental, putting all your stuff in storage, finding a place to rent out there renting furniture for the year and working with new people on top of that. Way too much work."

"This is a once in a lifetime opportunity. It seemed like it was worth the effort to me."

"I guess but then you just have to leave and go somewhere after that, and you don't even know where that is. So, you gave up the known for the unknown. We think it's crazy."

"I thought you said you all were proud of me."

"Kind of but we also think you are making a mistake."

"Let me get this straight, I get selected to be a part of a prestigious fellowship with a renowned research company, live in Santa Monica California for a year with an apartment that is a block away from the beach and it is crazy to take this opportunity because I signed a mobility agreement that says they can send me anywhere after this year is up?"

"Yep."

"Well, considering I lived in Oklahoma City for 12 years, in the middle of tornado alley with mostly white people I can't really think of much worse can you?"

"I don't know I am just saying it's somewhat ridiculous that you even thought to apply but good for you for believing you had a shot. Look where it got you!"

I want to walk out and drive back to my parents' house, get the girls, and leave right now but since we are scheduled to leave in the morning, I will endure a few more moments.

I am not an early riser except when it's time to leave my parents' house. I take forever to get down here and then right at sunrise I am up, girls are feed and bags are in the car. This morning is no different though my dad did try to convince me to stay another day to have one of my tires checked. He noticed a gash in the back passenger tire though there is no hole or air leaking. He said it was foolish to continue my drive to California with this tire not checked and I informed him we had made it eight hours from Virginia to here and it was fine so no worries. He wasn't happy with my nonchalant attitude about it and proceed to cuss me out and call me a fucking fool. I wanted to tell him I'd much rather take my chances with a tire blow out than spend one more day with him, but I kept quiet. I am not sure that his concern was so much about my safety as it was about him being right and after showing up in my new/used Range Rover he was looking for something to be wrong with it. In either case he walked off, went to bed and is now standing outside in his pajamas and robe with my mom saying their goodbyes to the girls. I reach to give them each a hug and they extend their arms for an extended pat on the back. It reminds me of all the times I used to try to give my family hugs when I was a little girl.

Our family was a television watching crew and, on the nights, when we had the back-to-back shows like *Alice* and *The Jeffersons* I would get up during the commercials and attempt to hug everyone. First my sister who was sitting on the floor next to me. She would turn away and then get up to get something from the kitchen. Next my dad who was always spit shinning his boots on the couch. I would give him a hug and a kiss on the check, and he wouldn't skip a beat with his boot shining never looking up never reciprocating never even a thank you. Then my mom who was always crocheting. She sat in the armchair working her crochet magic for another throw blanket. I would save her for last as she rounded out the living room. Same thing, hug and kiss and not once did she ever look up from her working -just kept crocheting. I must believe this is partly where my feelings of rejection, insecurities and lack of self love came from though interestingly I don't think I ever bothered to share this during my many therapy sessions.

But I digress as I tend to do. I accept their pats on the back and get in the car. There is always a huge since of relief when I back out of their driveway and today is no different. I don't bother to glance back and wave. I am now fixated on coffee and a greasy breakfast sandwich. Our first stop will be Memphis so here we go!

Facebook, July 5, 2015
Made it to Memphis! Celebrated the 4th with my family then hit the road this morning...ready for food and bed!

Facebook, July 5, 2015
Question??? Anyone know what happens to all the new bottles of ketchup after they are barely used? Seems like a waste...but I get that it's room service so packets would be tacky

Am I am really intrigued by these little bottles, or am I just whipped from the drive here? I was so thankful to leave my parents' house this morning. Even Cleo and Sophie were ready to go. They always are. As soon as they see me packing up our things, they race to the front door and wait, tails wagging. Once we head out the door, they are dragging me to the car, happy to hop in and get gone! I think it's very telling when dogs are ecstatic to leave a home. I am sure they know I've been unhappy during our visit, and they want me to get my happy back, which they know occurs as soon as we back out of the driveway as it did this morning.

Facebook, July 6, 2015
Late checkout = late arrival to Oklahoma City. We are pooped!! But as I was driving through . . . oh my goodness even in the dark I can see some cool changes over the last eight years! Shout out to my Tinker crew!

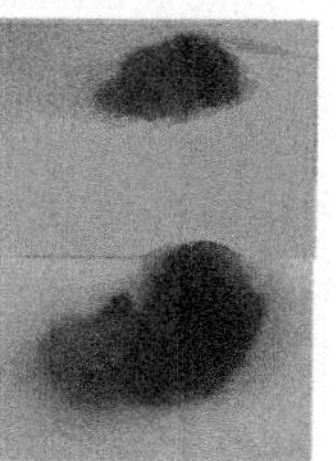

I am fairly sure I should feel something. Anything but alas, not a damn thing. I think Oklahoma broke the shit out of me, and although I have mad love for my friends and co-workers here, I am happy to be in and out of this town in one day. I allowed the same man to crack, break and fuck up my heart for ten years. That's all on me of course. That lack of self-love will fuck you up big time. Just the same, I have my walls up when I'm in this city and there's no breaking them, not even to meet up with old friends for a quick drink.

He reached out to me after I moved to the DMV. He called and hung up like a middle schooler. When he finally left a message, it was whack, but I seriously considered taking him back. That was the first time I sought a therapist. I relented to the fact that I must be broken to even consider taking that asshole back.

Therapy worked. I recall the day I told him I couldn't be with him again. I told him I had been seeing a therapist, and funny enough he got angry. He said, "I knew if you saw someone about us you wouldn't want to be with me again!"

No shit. But I have to think: if he knew he was that fucked-up, he would know he should be alone and leave his fucked-upness to himself. But, just like Dan, the fucked-up ones tend to seek the fucked-up ones. Just last year he sent me an email apologizing. He said he'd always loved me but didn't know how to show it. I wrote back and said I never loved him. I was desperately looking for someone to love me but was certain any breathing male would have done the trick. He then wanted to quote some Bible scriptures (though he was not a devout Christian), to which I thanked him and wished him well. I must admit, hearing from him was a red flag that I was not over my anger about our relationship, so I decided for Lent this year to give up my anger for him, for myself, and for the whole mess. I tend to stretch the concept of Lent into whatever works for me. I am a United Methodist, and we give up things, not meat like Catholics, but I don't know that my pastor would agree with giving up anger. I do think it worked, or maybe I was too busy packing and getting ready for this move that I just forgot about him again. If that's the case, yay for me. I can relive my fucked-up past sometime in the future.

Facebook, July 7, 2015
Just rolled into Albuquerque!
The odometer reads 2200
miles for this trip from VA to
SC to TN to OK to NM! This is an impressive road trip! Almost there!!!

I think I have checked the girls and I into the Bates Motel! This place sucks! I have done great so far in that every hotel along the way was up to our upper middle-class standards. But this place, oh no! It's not even a hotel, it's a remodeled motel – you know, where the room doors are on the outside of the building. The room smells and I am having a tough time deciding which of these two worn out beds we should sleep in tonight. Everything in the bathroom is rusty – even the towels have stains on them. I'll be skipping the shower tonight. I'm only traveling with my two girls, and I think they will be fine with me being un-fresh until we get to Phoenix tomorrow. There's nothing to eat in the nearby vicinity, and it's almost sunset so I am not comfortable leaving and coming back after dark. My goal is to take the girls out for a quick walk (and hope they can sleep through night with no potty breaks) in the condemned-looking parking lot that borders what appears to be abandoned homes, feed them, and eat this orange and apple my mom packed for me the other day. Though she says hurtful things and calls me fat, she still goes out of her way to pack food for me before I leave their house – fruit, nuts, cookies, all done out of love, I guess, but boy, if she could only see that it's such a contradiction to the words coming out of her mouth. For now, I will just have to accept it, packed snacks, and her secret goodnights where she acts civil towards me.

As I am walking the girls, my mind can't help but wander to Dan. I haven't heard from him, even though I've been texting him every day. He said to text him, to let him know how the trip was going. Of course, he didn't say he'd respond, but I kind of thought that was the point. I'll be sure to text him again tonight.

Facebook, July 8, 2015
Made it to Phoenix!!! It is SOOO hot! Too many years on the East Coast has desensitized me to 100+ degree weather! Gave up sightseeing and came back to my very cool hotel room.

It is hot as hellafockey! Who lives here on purpose? Today was a short 400-mile drive, so since we got here early and are staying downtown, I thought I'd do some sightseeing. I didn't make it two blocks. The temperature is 105 degrees, and it just feels like Hell. Granted, I have no clue what the hell Hell feels like but if Hell is hotter than this then I need to get my shit together!

My heart was breaking for my baby girls. I am worried they are going to develop blisters on their paws from the short walk. If it's 105 degrees, I can only imagine the sidewalk feels like fire. There is little grass around here, but I am guessing this is true for most of the state. But, as always, Cleo and Sophie were little troopers – not seeming to have a care in the world. Man, I love them so much.

Facebook, July 9, 2015
We are done!!! We are in Beautiful Santa Monica! Thanks to all of you for your thoughts and prayers! Looking forward to a momentous year at Big Brains, Inc.!

We've arrived! It's early afternoon, and a phenomenally beautiful sunny day. There was a mix-up with the move-in date for the apartment, and since I have to report to Big Brains on Monday, I booked us a room at Ocean View Resort. To date, this will be the fanciest hotel I've stayed in.

I pull into the driveway of the hotel where a bellhop greets us. I'm exhausted, but relieved. I am a ball of emotions, but I must keep moving forward. All I want to do is get the car unpacked, take the girls for a quick walk, get a good meal and a good sleep. I still have to arrange for the utilities in the apartment to be turned on, and I need to report to work on Monday, and I have a good two-and-a-half days to become familiar again with Santa Monica. It's been a few years since I was last here on TDY (Temporary Duty), and for those trips, I didn't venture past the 3rd Street Promenade.

"Good afternoon! Welcome Ocean View Resort."

I smile and I can feel my eyes sparkling with delight through my sunglasses. I can tell this type of attention is already giving me a big head.

"Thank you!"

"Let me help you. Will you need everything from the vehicle?" The bellhop is an older gentleman with what sounds like an Italian accent. I am guessing his age to be mid-sixties, but only because of his silver hair and a faint set of wrinkles cast around his tan face. His body does not match his face. Though older, he is built like a body builder, and his muscles are pressed firmly against his uniform. Damn, he is sexy!

"Unfortunately, yes, as we will be staying for a week."

"No problem, ma'am."

I pop the trunk and he begins to unload the car. As he does, I go to the back seat to unbuckle the girls. As usual, they have been the best companions. These two are truly my road dogs.

I enter the hotel with Cleo, Sophie and the bellhop who is pushing our belongings behind us. My weave is on point, and I'm dressed in a royal blue maxi dress and brown wedge sandals. You can't tell me I'm not Elle Woods from *Legally Blonde* – only I'm reversing it, arriving on the West Coast rather than the East.

As I reach the counter, the bellhop hands me two bottles of water.

"For the dogs, ma'am. You'll find sparkling water in the room for you."

"Why, thank you." My smile could shatter the windows in this place. First day in California at this fancy hotel, and the bellhop gives me free water for the dogs. I feel like a rich person. I feel like part of the elite. Plus, pulling up in my baby Range Rover has added to my assumed upper-echelon status.

Marco, the bellhop, has gotten us settled into our room. I am impressed how he took all this junk out of the car and got it on one of those little carts. As I'm tipping him (I hope ten dollars is a good tip), he's handing me more bottles of water for the girls. I'm feeling special. I'm feeling a little bit above myself. I'm in this impressive hotel by the beach and I have a bellhop hooking me up with extra sundries!

"Thanks again for your help, Marco."

"You are welcome, Ms. McClure. Enjoy your stay."

Life is good right now. I can't wait to get the girls out for a walk, find something good to eat for lunch, and take a short nap. I can't rest long, though, as I must get everything going to turn on the utilities in the apartment. I want everything done as soon as possible because I know this year is going to fly, and I want to get settled quickly so that I can really enjoy myself. Thank you, God, for this opportunity!

As we enter the elevator to head out for a walk, a wave of sadness overcasts my *Lifestyles of the Rich and Famous* moment. Dan. I thought he cared about me, but he's blown me off since I started heading west. I've texted every day of our journey, and nothing until last night in Phoenix. I'm quite sure the only reason I received a response was because I played the "woe is me" card. I sent him a text telling him I was nervous about coming out here:

I've been trying to contact you all week and nothing. I'm heading out to the other side of the country to do this new thing. I don't know anyone out here and this is a big deal to me. I needed your support. I thought you wanted to know how I was doing each day. Why are you ignoring me? I'm all alone and I just need a friend.

He texted me back a pep talk:

Sorry, Ava, been busy. Showing homes and making a name for myself in the real estate game. You're going to do fine. You're Ava-Flava! Starting something new is not hard—you just have to start. Take care.

The day before I left, he said he didn't want to be with anyone else but me, and here we are a week later, and he's ghosted me. Though he did also say let's turn off our friends with benefits mode for this year so perhaps ghosting is not ghosting but getting on with his life. In either case, I'm determined to not let this ruin my time out here. I'm excited to meet the other fellows in a couple days and move into my apartment a few days after that.

I feel somewhat unsure and insecure, but I feel pretty damn good, too. This is my year and I'm going to make the best of it. I'm going to enjoy everything there is to do in California! To hell with Dan's ass! We've parted ways before and I didn't die. This time will be no different. Maybe it will be easier since we are on opposite sides of the country.

The girls and I head down Main Street and begin our walk (I'm thankful the hellish heat of Phoenix didn't give them blisters on their paws). I am blessed to be here. I'm in California for a year — how could it be anything but a blessing?

Facebook, July 10, 2015
Ok so yesterday I gave you a sad view of Santa Monica due to exhaustion 😄 but this morning's view as I was walking the dogs is a much better site.

Day two here and after being on the phone with the cable, gas, and electric companies it's time for me to head out and have a nice lunch. I can't eat in this place every day 'cause I ain't rich. I had room service for breakfast to not leave Cleo and Sophie alone yet, but they will be fine for an hour or so. Time to see what's out here in beautiful, sunny Santa Monica, California.

It doesn't hurt that I'm in familiar territory. The couple of TDY trips to Big Brains over the years makes this move less daunting, though I did up and move my ass from Oklahoma to Virginia without much thought eight years ago. Back then, I was moving as a reaction. This time it's deliberate. Well, mostly. I did apply for this fellowship, and I wanted this opportunity, but I was still shocked as shit when I found out I was selected.

I'm going to head over to the mall. I can't mess that up since I know how to get there, and anything from the food court will do me just fine.

"Okay, babies, see you later! I'm going to run out and get some food for myself, but I won't be gone long. I love you! Be good, and no barking. Love you, love you, love you! Bye, bye!"

I feel so peaceful moving down the street and weaving my way through crowds headed towards the beach and the pier. As I make my way up to the mall, I pass a man dressed as Batman. He seems pleasant. I can't say I recall seeing people dressed in costumes during any of my other visits. No one else seems concerned, must be normal. His costume is dirty, and he is walking by and waving at folks. Interesting or it just bizarre? Or am I the only one seeing this? I have been having thoughts about this device during my drive out here. I was convinced I just had too much time on my hands as I was driving solo with no one to talk to – the girls are great travel companions, but they don't offer any verbal stimulation. As we were driving through Texas I was sure I was experiencing heat mirages but then I started thinking what if it was this device? This non-working could be eating a hole in my brain device? So, what if I am the only one seeing this Batman dude? Wait, no as I keep staring at him I see a family pointing at him and waving so this has be real, right?

Okay, you're good or maybe not but at least Batman is real! I continue my way to mall. This is all new and yet curiously familiar, since I've been here before. It's as though I am in a trance. I'm sure things will really kick in once I start work next week and get settled into the apartment. The mall is a familiar place. I remember the first time I was here a few years ago. I vowed to come back with tons of money, able to shop in any of the stores. While I don't have tons of money, I can eat in the food court and this little sandwich shop is perfect. Cranberry and turkey panini with a smoothie sounds great.

While I'm waiting for my order to be called, I pull out my phone and begin typing a text to Marva.

Made it here! Don't get too good on that pole without me this year!

I hear my number called and walk up to get my food. As I turn to sit again, my body freezes. Now my heart is pounding, and I feel myself smiling. This can't be real, can it? I look across the food court, marveling that I am here. I am here. Not someone else. Me, damn it! I once won a coloring book in the second grade. Fast forward thirty-four years later, and I feel like I've won the lottery. I am going to live the hell out of this next year!

Facebook, July 13, 2015
DMVers!!! My friend will be in town this weekend! Her workout is awesome! It works your entire body, and the music is so great you feel like your jammin in the Motherland!!!

I have not yet been gone a full month and I'm already missing Freakazoid. Before my love affair with Freakazoid, there was AfricaJam. This class was everything. The African beats took me away for an hour twice a week and allowed me to be free! I'll be sure to check out the local gyms this week so I can get that personal trainer I promised myself. This year I am going to take care of me. Something I stopped doing a few years ago. I used to work out every day, had a six pack, and ran a few times a week then I just stopped. Dan likes to point out the remnants of my muscles. He too has lost his sexy body over the years, yet I say nothing to him about it. I know I am wanting to get back in shape to show him how good I can look. Man, I must admit therapy has worked in the sense that I am completely aware of my feelings and subsequent behavior but damn I don't do anything to improve my life. I guess that's why I should have taken Dr. Smith up on her offer to connect me with a therapist out here but just for this year, just for a small moment of what I am sure will be a lifetime of therapy I need a break.

Facebook, July 13, 2015
Friday was my 20th anniversary with the Air Force! How great is God that He is blessing me to spend my 20th year like this! Finally made it to the beach! So yesterday I headed out to treat myself to dinner and wandered onto the pier and somehow found myself on the beach sitting on the warm sand and thanking God for such wonderful scenery and His blessing me to have this career opportunity in THIS PLACE! The sound of the ocean was so soothing, and the warmth of the sun was sending me sunshine hugs!

I can't believe I spent my twentieth year nowhere near a DoD installation. I still can't believe I'm here. Before I left Shawshank, my

office gave me my twenty-year pin. Gen. Deeds made a point of saying, "Well, Ava. Twenty years means a lot! It means you're wrapping up your federal career. It's time to start thinking about what's next." Clearly, he has no clue the Federal Employees Retirement System (FERS) will to not be signing my freedom papers for another sixteen years – minimum. Plus, I signed a five-year continuation of service agreement as part of this fellowship, so even if I up and left, I'd owe sixty thousand dollars. However, I am eligible to defer my retirement, so maybe I should start thinking about how I can swing this financially after my five-year commitment. I have digressed to a whole other topic. Truthfully, the topic of freedom is always swirling around in my head. It is my mission to achieve it.

Not a peep from Dan, but I'm surviving. Sitting here on this warm sand watching the waves crashing against the shore is like having any level of emotion wash away from my brain. I feel the breeze with the wetness of the ocean tingling my face, and I smile. If only I could be here all day, I'd never have a care in the world.

2

Big Brains, Inc.

Maybe I should be more nervous than this, but for some reason I'm not. I have walked the dogs. I'm dressed as casually as I can be, as it was noted in the handbook I received about this corporation that they're extremely casual. The hotel is just a five-minute walk from Big Brains which will make for a nice stroll. This is going to be a good day.

"Bye, babies! See you later! Be good, and no barking!"

We've still got four more days in this hotel, and so far, so good. I am getting too comfortable with this lifestyle. Every time I step out to walk the dogs, we are greeted by the staff and there is always an expensive vehicle parked out front with a bellhop either unloading or loading the contents. I'm thankful I listened to Dan. While my baby Range isn't a Maserati or a Tesla, it is a Range Rover, and it makes me feel as though I belong to this elite world.

This morning, there's a posh looking couple waiting for the bellhop to finish loading their luggage into their white Mercedes AMG GT Coupe. Damn, that thing is nice! I'm a fan of nice vehicles and I know this one is new to the market. I didn't even know it was out for purchase yet, but who in the hell knows who this couple is and what type of connections they have.

I long for a life like this. I know money doesn't buy happiness, but I have to believe if money weren't an issue I could spend the time to get to a better place emotionally. A place where Dan is not even a tiny spot in my brain.

I pass by the couple and the woman smiles at me. I smile back. I think it was a "hello, rich person" greeting. If only she knew I was a lowly federal employee, who can only afford to stay in this hotel because of her tax dollars, and mine. Actually, I can just say my tax dollars. After twenty years of being single and filing taxes, I'm certain this extended TDY has been one hundred percent financed by me.

As I make my way across Ocean Avenue and head up Olympic Drive, I see a coffee shop on the corner. Nice! I haven't been to Big Brains in a few years and this part of the city has changed considerably to include Tongva Park. Since arriving the other day, I've only been west on Ocean Avenue – the beach and the mall. I've noticed the park, but everything else over here is brand new to me.

There's a familiar face. The receptionist at this corporation. I've seen her before the few times I've come out on trips. I'm sure she sees so many people that she doesn't remember me, and her look at this very moment shows she indeed does not remember me. It's all good though. I'm ready to start this new adventure and ready to shake off the last few days of driving through the hot Arizona heat, and Dan's dumb ass. I'm ready to make this year absolutely fabulous!

"Hello! Welcome to Big Brains!"

"Hello! My name is Ava McClure. I am here to meet Nancy. I am part of the fellowship program."

"Oh, hello Ava! Yes, Nancy said to look out for you. Let me give her a call. Hello Nancy, Ava McClure is here. Okay I will let her know."

The receptionist continues her conversation with Nancy on a different subject so I back away from her desk and look around. It's been a few years since I was last here, but everything looks the same.

The building is very airy and open with windows from floor to ceiling. I see a few people coming in for work and I am remembering how casual they are here. It's Monday and people are wearing shorts, Hawaiian shirts, and sandals. We received a welcome package noting the work attire was casual and I am doing my best to fit in, but I can see I am overdressed in one of my modern day/throwback Jackie O looks. I am wearing a two-toned dress that is lemon lime on the top, off white on the bottom with slender gold chain serving as a belt. My shoe choice is open toed two-inch gold heels. While this may be a great casual Friday look at Shawshank it considerably dressy for a Monday morning at Big Brains. I recall during those visits in the past being dressed in business suits and my signature super high heels. It didn't bother me then because I was expected to look this way but being as I am now "one of them" for the next year I want to blend in as much as possible. I'll have to try to take it down a bit more tomorrow.

"Ava!"

I turn to see a small framed Asian woman waving at me as she exits the elevator. I was so deep in my thoughts I had not noticed the receptionist was no longer on the phone and Nancy is now down here to meet me.

"Hi Nancy! It's nice to meet you!"

"Nice to meet you too! Oh, you are just going to love it here! I have everything already for you upstairs!"

I give a smile and wave to the receptionist and follow Nancy into the elevator.

"So, how was the drive out here?"

"It was great, I stretched the trip out to five days, so it was very pleasant."

"Oh, that's smart! So many folks get caught up in trying to drive straight through or stopping once, maybe twice but I say why rush, this place isn't going anywhere!"

We exit the elevator and I follow Nancy to her desk.

"Just need to give you this." She hands me a binder with a cover entitled "Welcome to Big Brains, Inc."

"This is everything you'll need to know mostly about the other businesses we are affiliated with so make sure you check it out. There are some great discounts you can take advantage of."

"Thank you, I sure will."

"Now, on to your office."

We walk a few feet, and she opens the door to one of the offices. It's been years since I had my own office- 2007 to be exact when I left Oklahoma. Cubicle life has been my new normal and I think I adapted okay over the years, but I am going to love this privacy.

"We will have the ergonomic specialist come by later today to do an assessment to ensure everything is adjusted correctly for you. You are short like me so you may need a lift for your feet. It will help keep your back aligned."

What in the heck? No one has ever cared about my ergonomic needs in my entire 20 years of working for the Air Force. But okay I'll accept an ergonomic assessment!

The rest of the morning is filled with the basic administrative things, obtaining a badge, getting my laptop which by the way came with an hour tutorial, and a tour of the building. Coming here in the past I've only been to the conference rooms on the first floor so seeing the entire building was impressive. The open airy feel continues past the lobby and extends to the entire space. The floor where my office is located is bright with the entire wall full of windows. While all the private offices in this area are not on the window side there is still an abundance of light glimmering through my glass door. This is nothing like Shawshank where the only windows are on the E Ring and the only people who can see out of those windows are the most important ones – Secretaries, Chiefs and other 4 Star Generals and Senior Executive Service members. Whenever I was in one of their offices I would stop for a second and take in the view.

"Knock, knock."

I look up from my computer to see Nancy with two young ladies.

"Ava, meet your fellow Fellows Jane and Mandy!"

The two give a hello in unison and I smile as I stand to give them and give a hello back and handshakes.

"You will have plenty of time to get to know each other this year but for now I am going to get these ladies their badges and laptops!"

"Okay, nice meeting you! See you soon!" Hum, two white chicks. This is going to be interesting. My mind drifts back to working with Marcy in OSD. Not fun times but that's stereotyping white females and that's not cool. We'll see.

I turn to sit back down and here a knock on my door. I turn to see an older white man in the doorway with a notebook and what appears to be a toolbox.

"Hello, I am Henry the ergonomic specialist."

"Oh, hello! Thank you for stopping by!"

I move to the side and to let Henry look at my set up. As he does so I am finally stopping to look at it myself, plus the office in total. It's nice, maybe five feet by ten feet. The walls are bare except for one whiteboard but Nancy said I can hang artwork or request another whiteboard or corkboard for notes and get this, the maintenance crew will come hang the artwork for me. The desk where my computer is runs along one of the walls and against the other wall is a small table with two chairs which makes for a nice meeting space and just behind them is a two-drawer file cabinet. Everything white which allows for the brilliant sun to shine in and give the space such a warm glow.

"Do you mind taking a seat? I would like to see if we need to get you a new chair or a lift for your feet."

"Sure."

I sit in my chair and Henry spins me around to take a look.

"The chair is good, but you need a lift. I'll be back with one for you in a few. How about your arms? Can you reach the keyboard okay and is the keyboard working for you?"

"Yes, I can and yes I've always wanted an ergonomic keyboard, so this is wonderful!"

"Perfect! Let me go get that lift for you and you'll be set for the year."

"Thank you!"

I watch Henry leave my office (my office!) and return to my chair. Yep, this is going to be a damn good year!

3

Move In Day

Our bags are packed…again. We've been waiting for the bellhop to arrive at our room. I'm looking forward to getting settled in the apartment and settling into my life here.

"Good morning, Ms. McClure!"

"Good morning!"

I step aside and allow the bellhop to begin loading our bags onto the cart. I have the girls by my side on their leashes, ready to do my Elle Woods exit from the room.

"I hope you've had an enjoyable stay."

"Oh, yes it was quite wonderful."

After only a week, I've acclimated to the luxury lifestyle. I can hear an air of elitism in my voice.

"Such a marvelous hotel. We will indeed miss it, but it's time for us to get settled in our new place."

"Very nice, ma'am. We do hope to see you again soon."

"Oh, most definitely. I'm sure I'll be back for a weekend getaway."

I know I'm lying, but somehow it feels as though I'm not. I want it to be true. The concierge noted the other evening that many folks staying here live in L.A. and come down to the beach for just that – a few days away. Ah, the rich. Considering L.A. is right down the street and Santa Monica is part of L.A. County, it seems absurd, but heck if I had the money to burn, I'd do it.

I am a believer in manifesting what you want. Take this apartment, for example. I looked at the photos online, noticed some balconies had rails and others were solid concrete walls. I knew I would need a unit with the solid concrete wall for the girls' safety. I took a screenshot of a balcony with the concrete wall and used it as my wallpaper until I secured the unit. When the property manager sent the photos of my unit, there it was – the concrete balcony. I've even done this when Dan ghosts me and it always works. I use a picture of him as my wallpaper on my phone and he reappears. Though, one might note, he always *reappears*, meaning he's always *disappearing*, so perhaps this is not the best example.

I've checked out of the hotel and am driving down the street to our new place. It's still early, so I'm able to secure a parking spot across from where we live on Santa Monica Boulevard. I get Cleo and Sophie out of the car, and we head to the apartment building. The building was a movie theater at one point. After an earthquake a few years ago, it was converted into a boutique apartment building.

Wow, this feels way too normal. Just another day, taking possession of an apartment one block from the beach.

As we exit the elevator, I see the property manager Judy waving at me.

"Welcome, Ava!"

"Hi Judy, how are you?"

"I'm great!"

"Ready to move in?"

"Yes, we are."

"Oh! They are adorable!"

Judy is bending over, allowing Cleo and Sophie to sniff her hands. She pats both on the head and raises up to greet me again. She is gorgeous. She's about five feet, two inches with jet black hair. Her eyes are an interesting hazel with specks of blue, and she's wearing a plum-colored lipstick which matches her floral print dress. She is rocking what appears to be a five-inch heel and is beaming from ear to ear.

"I have everything ready for you to finish the paperwork so you guys can get settled in."

"Great, thanks!"

She motions for us follow her down the hall and opens the office door.

"There are just a few more signatures I need for the lease and the deposit check, and then we're done!"

I smile and sign, not reading any of it, and hand Judy the check. She hands me the keys and squats down to pet the girls. Sophie is loving the head pats and Cleo has rolled over for a tummy rub. I am thankful for these two. My road dogs! They've traveled from Oklahoma to Virginia and now to California. They are my constants. My rocks.

Judy breaks from head pats and tummy rubs and stands up with incredible ease. I'm sure I could not rise that quickly from a squat in a pair of stilettos.

"Sorry, I could love on these two all day! Here are your keys and the move-in inspection form. You can return it within the next two days."

"Thanks for everything, Judy. I really appreciate your support with this transition."

"My pleasure! And welcome to Santa Monica!"

With keys in hand, the girls and I head to the elevator and select five. I am overjoyed we are on the top floor! No noisy neighbors thumbing around above us. Having lived in the house in Alexandria for so many years, the thought of apartment living was a little daunting, but when Judy noted she had a fifth-floor unit available in my price range I immediately said yes. I recall my Shawshank pod mate, Al, turning and giving a big smile after I'd told him about my dislike for apartment living while searching the internet one day.

"Apartment living is the best! You get to live around so many interesting people."

"I'm fairly certain I classify as a hermit, so that in no way appeals to me."

"Ava, you're nowhere close to being a hermit."

"That's only because I have to come out in public to make a living."

"Touché."

We exit on the fifth floor and walk down the hall. I am in heaven! To my left is the rooftop patio, and I must take a quick glance. I walk the girls over and stare in wonderment. There are serval patio sectionals with yellow cushions and bright orange ottomans. There are a few potted plants, but otherwise the area is nondescript yet L.A.-ish. And there it is! The beach and the park I know we will spend an enormous amount of time in. I can smell the ocean breeze from here – or at least I believe I can. I'll be here for months and will still be in disbelief.

I shake my head and come back to my senses. The cable guy and the furniture rental company will be here within the hour.

"Okay, girls let's see our new home!"

We walk a few more feet and land at apartment 504. I open the door, walk in, and drop the leashes. Our boxes arrived a few days prior. Judy was kind enough to allow the UPS guy to deliver them to the apartment even though it wasn't officially ready for me to me in to. The girls get busy sniffing every nook and cranny while I head for the balcony doors. I open them and smile. I have absolutely no view, except for what looks like the top of a few store rooftops on the Promenade, but that's okay as we at least have some outdoor space.

Cleo and Sophie have now joined me. While they can't see a thing because of the concrete wall, I can see they are happy about their balcony as well. I turn around take it all in. It's a small unit at just over 500 square feet, but we don't need any more than this. Just past the front door is a small closet with a stackable washer and dryer, and just beyond that is the bathroom, which is oddly huge with a wonderfully large garden tub. Across from the bathroom is the tiny kitchen which sits in front of the living room and dining area. Just beyond the dining area is the bedroom, which Judy said had a partial ocean view. I walk inside the bedroom and find the narrow window. It indeed has an ocean view. I see a palm tree, a blip of sand and a tiny spot that would be the ocean. Nonetheless, it's an ocean view and I smile.

My blissful content is disrupted by my phone ringing. It's the cable guy.

Two hours later, the cable guy has finished, flirted, and left his number. The furniture rental crew have come and gone. I'm sitting on a lime green sofa watching Cleo and Sophie nap next to me. I picked the most bizarre sofa, or at least bizarre compared to the Midwestern style of furniture I tossed prior to moving out here. When I was looking at the sofas online, this green struck me as fresh and new. I knew it would set the tone for this year. I'll have to buy some cheap patio furniture so we can take full advantage of our outdoor living space. Then we'll be good to go.

Facebook, July 21, 2015
Just got my gym membership and a personal trainer! So Mike no one can replace you, but I wanted to kick my butt while I'm out here, so I went back to a trainer. And only you will tell me to stop complaining and grunt and fart it out oh and my fav...tell it to Oprah!!!

I elected for a membership at We Are Fitness as it's right around the corner from my apartment and it was one of the companies Big Brain partners with, so the discount made for an easy decision. Surely, I'll be diligent with my workouts since it's only a five-minute walk. My trainer is young and super cute. His name is Greg. Maybe six-two with red hair and bright green eyes and every inch of him is muscular. This will be a nice treat for myself – both the work out and getting to look at Greg three days a week. My first session is tomorrow evening and I'm looking forward to the experience.

Before heading back to my apartment, I decide to grab something for dinner. As I pull out my phone to see what's nearby, I notice I have a text from Dan.

"Hey! Hope you're settling in okay out there. Hit me up when you get a second."

He's only texting because he knows I'll be heading that way in a few days. I can't believe him. I'm heading back to town, and he wants to hook up? But otherwise, he doesn't give a crap about what in the hell is going on with me.

I toss my phone back in my bag and decide on a salad since I'm standing in front of a place called Salad Garden.

As I head up to the apartment, I feel compelled to respond to Dan, but only to cuss him out. I toss my salad in the refrigerator and take the girls out for their evening walk.

Cleo and Sophie are little stars out here. They get so much attention, it's strange. I, of course, know how incredibly cute they are, but to have people stopping us, wanting to say hi to them, some even wanting to take pictures with them – it's crazy, but if I ever get their book series written this could really be their life. I stopped working on it again. This is sad since it's a children's book series and should not take long to crank out - at least the first book. I am certain I will work on it this year and who knows, perhaps make some connections while I am out here and get it published!

We've made it to our favorite part of Palisades Park with a comfy palm tree that seems to greet us as we approach. Maybe it's crazy, but I feel quite drawn to this tree. We sit here for prolonged periods of time and just chill. It's only been two weeks, but we've got this park as our go-to place, and this tree as our sacred spot. It's like the DMV version of our Zen time on Mount Vernon Trail, only we can have this time every day since it's a block away. We don't have to wait for the weekend to take the drive to get to Zen.

Sitting here feeling tranquil, I pull out my phone. I'm not a fan of taking my phone when I walk the dogs as it's my downtime, but I'm still very much in tourist-mode and find myself taking pictures of the ocean every chance I get, so the phone has accompanied us for the last two weeks.

I pull up Dan's name and dial his number.

"Ava-Flava!"

"Hey."

"What's up? How's L.A.?"

"I wouldn't know, I'm in Santa Monica."

"It's all the same. So, how's it going?"

"Good."

"Are you pissed at me or something?"

"Nope. What's up?"

"You sound pissed. Anyway, I wanted to see when you are going to be back in town. You said sometime later this month and the month's almost over."

I should lie and tell him I was already there and not mess with his ass when I get into town in a few days.

"Yeah, I'm flying out on Sunday. We have an Icebreaker (an uncomfortable social gathering the night before the start of a conference or other event that is designed, I believe, with good intention but always proves to be mediocre) that evening from five to seven, and then I'm free. The rest of the week, I am free in the evenings after five according to the agenda.

"Cool. So, maybe I can come see you Sunday night. What hotel are you staying at?"

"The Inn in Crystal City."

"Okay. I'll give you a call Sunday. I'm looking forward to seeing you, Ava. I'm already missing you."

"Really?"

"Yes, really."

"I thought you wanted to take a break from our arrangement while I was out here?"

"I did, but I still miss you and we are still friends, right?"

"Sure, of course."

"Anyway, I want you, Ava, and I want to see you while you are out here."

What is he saying? He doesn't want to take a break? Or that he does but, since I'm going to be in town, let's make an exception? Probably the latter, I'm sure, but I won't ask. Asking questions is how

I managed to end our arrangement just days before I came out here. Be freakin' positive, Ava, damn.

"I'm looking forward to seeing you, too."

"Take care and have a safe trip."

"Thanks. See you in few days."

This is hopeful. Maybe he just needed some time to think through things and he now realizes we are perfect together and he doesn't want to end things while I'm out here.

Beaming with delight, I rest my head against the tree and close my eyes. Positive thoughts, Ava, positive thoughts. Who am I fooling? I can' hold a positive thought about this insane relationship, arrangement, hook-up or whatever it is. This is because I am well aware of the truth and that is this shit with Dan is never going to go anywhere. Maybe I should be in therapy this year.

Facebook, July 22, 2015
My face is smiling but my body wants to collapse and vomit...awesome workout!!! Just like the good old days! Can't wait for my next session!

Greg is kicking my ass, though I wish I could magically lose this weight overnight. I'm less than a week away from seeing Dan, and I want to look as good as possible. I could have loss weight while I was back in the DMV. Sure, I was at Freakazoid several times a week, but I was eating so much that all I was doing was maintaining my weight.

It seems though I shouldn't give a shit about how Dan views me, but of course I do.

4

Return to the DMV

Whenever I fly into Reagan airport, which is most times as I'm not a fan of Dulles (it was too far from my house), I'm always struck by those people who are looking out of the window, leaning on it trying to see the Pentagon. As much as I love having a window seat, I am not remotely interested in an aerial view of Shawshank. A couple times I've taken a peek, but I'm not impressed with the big ass building. If they only knew the crazy that resides inside, they wouldn't be so impressed.

Anyway, as soon as I get this week over, I can get back to my babies and back to Southern California living. My place is pretty much pulled together and there's nothing to do but go to work and live. I think I'm going to get back into my writing this year. It never leaves me, and I think this year I'll find the time to commit to it. I don't think I'm going to worry about the online pet store for my business. I will take advantage of being in the high-class L.A. area and see what I can glean from their doggy boutiques, daycares etc. There will be plenty of time for me to be an entrepreneur after I finish my year with Big Brains.

I always feel as though I've hit the jackpot when I walk into a hotel and there is no one at the check-in desk. I'm generally a patient person, and when I do have to wait it's not a big deal, yet there's this

YES moment when I can just step up and be helped. It feels like pure bliss.

"Good evening and welcome!"

"Hello, how are you?"

As the nice young man checks me in, I see the sign for my orientation group. I truly hate these Icebreakers. I'm not a fan of small talk and chit-chat. I've been at Big Brains for two weeks and have gotten to know the other Air Force Fellows, but there's only three of us at Big Brains. Maybe there will be others I've met during my career that I will recognize. Or, just maybe, Ava, this would serve as a good opportunity to meet new people – just a thought. Oh well, we'll see. I'm much more interested in getting this over with so I can see Dan later tonight and get to bed at a decent hour. The start time is ridiculously early at 7:00 AM, but it is what it is.

I've gone to my room, dropped off my luggage, changed and made a Facebook post. I can't believe I stayed off social media all these years.

Facebook, July 29, 2015
See that smiley face above that swanky looking midrise? That was my first home when I moved to the DMV. I am back this week for an orientation and my hotel room faces my first place. Something about this seems like a sign from God to me - reminding me of all the great blessings over the last eight years and a reminder that many more are to come. It's hard to believe eight years have come and gone since I left Oklahoma. It's been a wonderful journey and I'm looking forward to continuing the adventure!!!

So, I'm here at this Icebreaker. I see the other fellows from Big Brains. I'll just start this off by speaking with them.

"Hey, guys! How long have you been here?"

"Too long," sighs Jane.

Jane is going to be interesting this year. For the last two weeks, she's done nothing but joke about being here. She's not sure how she was selected and thinks her application for this fellowship should have been tossed in the trash. That's saying a lot, but I find that people like this are usually just deflecting from how great they think they are. Talking this way somehow humbles them to us regular people. Not to mention Jane is tall, blonde and looks out-of-place as a government employee. She looks like she should be walking a runway and making tons of money with some cosmetic company, not reliant on a government salary that comes with no glitz or glamour.

"Oh, well I hope to show my face for about an hour and then leave."

"We can do that?" Mandy asks with a confused looked on her face.

Mandy is the other Fellow. She is focused, and it's clear she is here to fill a square and get promoted. She is a Lt Col and is awaiting the announcement of her Col select status. She is visibly disappointed she will be spending the year with us, as the elite don't do these types of fellowships. They do elitist type shit, like go War College at Fort McNair in D.C.

Mandy is about five feet tall, like me, and has short brown hair. She is nondescript and has no style whatsoever. I feel bad for her, and as I look around the room, I see it's a thing. The military do not know how to dress socially. Too many years in those uniforms, I guess. The room is a sea of khaki pants and button downs but with no flare, and no one is rocking a shoe that has anything to do with their outfit. It's like they all went to Macy's, but no one bothered to see how the mannequin was dressed. I chose to wear a tomato red wrap dress and a white linen jacket with quarter length sleeves. I opted for my favorite Anne Klein goldish/platinum two-inch sandals. A bit more than evening casual wear, but not boring as hell either.

I wander out with Mandy to the hall where there are some cheap appetizers and fix a small plate of food. I have no intentions of eating anything, but I think it looks less awkward if you are walking and holding a plastic plate of nasty food.

I run into a few folks I've seen around the Pentagon and make small talk with them for a few minutes. Once I notice a few people leaving, I causally pass a trashcan, dump my plate, and make my way back to my room.

Dan will be here in a about an hour, and I need to get dressed – out of this and into something a bit sexier.

In my room staring at the handful of casual clothes I brought for the week, I decide on a black strapless maxi dress and black Michael Kors flipflops. Dan has texted that he will be here at 8:00 and I've decided to dash over to the pizza place down the block and pick up dinner. This will be nice. It has to be. He did say he only wanted to be with me just a few weeks ago so me being gone and coming back for this orientation will make him see how much he misses me. It must, or not.

Dressed in my maxi dress, I head down to the lobby and out the door. I run into Mandy on my way out.

"Oh, don't you look cute."

She is giving a compliment but the look on her face says I look like a slut or something.

"Thanks."

"Meeting up with friends?"

"No. My boyfriend is coming over and I am going to pick up dinner for us down the street."

"Oh, cool. I'm going out with some friends that are stationed here. So glad I've never had to live here. This week will be more than enough for me."

"That's interesting. Yes, some love the DMV, and some hate it, but if you're moving up in your military career, it's my understanding this is the place to be – at the Headquarters." Yes, that was a dig but she's a little bitchy to me and I don't give a shit tonight.

"Oh, well yes, it is that's why I'm sure they'll send me here next though I know I will hate it."

"Of course. We'll have a good night!"

I don't give Mandy a chance to respond as I quickly turn to head out down the street. It feels good to be back. I've only been away for two weeks, and this feeling of familiarity is nice. Getting acclimated to the L.A. area has been easy but being out there with just Cleo and Sophie has proven a little lonely already, especially with Dan ghosting me.

As I'm walking, I see other Fellows who have made their way out of the Icebreaker and are roaming the streets of Crystal City aimlessly. I smile as I cross at 18th and Fern Street. At least I know where I'm going since this was my home.

As I enter the restaurant, it hits me. I didn't clean my booty. Dan loves to fuck in the ass. I'd better run over to the drug store and get an enema after I place my order.

This walk back to the hotel is draining me. The humidity is hell in July, and it doesn't help that I'm getting more nervous about seeing Dan.

As I approach the lobby, I see Jane.

"Hey, Ava!"

"Hi."

"That's a lot of food."

"Yeah, it's for Dan and me."

"Oh, that's great! I see so many people have their spouses and family here. That's so wonderful. I would have invited my husband, but he's out of the country right now. He files internationally."

"Yes, that's right, you mentioned that last week."

"Yeah, well, the best part is he has to come to visit me this year as he can fly anywhere with the airline. No excuses!"

"So true! Well, I'd better get upstairs."

"Okay, see you later!"

"See you!"

Maybe Dan will fly out and visit me. Maybe.

I make it back to my room and strip off my dress and panties to use the enema. I hate ass fucking and I think it should be illegal. Actually, I am quite sure it is illegal in some states. Who in the world thinks having something the size of a turd going into your ass is a good feeling? Hell, it doesn't feel so great when you shit so why have a reverse shit experience? I can tell it turns him on. I fake the pleasure and endure the pain and then usually shed a tear for how much I can't seem to get it together to love myself enough to leave all this shit with Dan behind.

After a quick shower I am feeling fresh, and I am back in my dress. I thought about changing into something else since it was so humid outside, but I am in my don't give a fuck mode after the enema.

I'm laying the food out as quickly as I can, and then I hear the knock on the door. I give myself a quick check in the bathroom mirror, pray all the liquid from the enema I just gave myself is out of my ass and head to the door.

"Ava-Flava!"

"Hey."

"Welcome back."

"Thanks, have a seat."

I motion for him to sit on the love seat in the living area of the suite. As he does, I check out his outfit. Why is he so damn sexy in anything he wears? Tonight, he's wearing a short sleeve red, white and blue checkered button-down shirt, khaki shorts, and old-style K-Swiss tennis shoes. Maybe it's the sexy/preppy thing that turns me on, but who am I kidding? Dan is sexy like this: in a business suit as a Senator's chief of staff, and in his flight suit when he's a reservist.

"Okay, so why are you nervous?"

"Am I?"

"Yeah, you are. It's just me."

"That it is. Thanks for coming over. We have an early start in the morning, so it helps to be here."

"No problem. It's nice to be in a hotel with you."

"I guess. Do you want anything to eat?"

I glance over at the table that's covered in boxes. I stuck with simple, basic items like flatbread and lettuce wraps.

"Nope, I'm good."

Dan is looking a bit nervous himself as he walks closer towards me. Before I can take a breath, he has wrapped his arms around my waist and has yanked my maxi dress down to my feet. I feel nothing and I'm sure why. How can I possibly have any excitement about this loveless but love you like a friend, bad sex arrangement? Nope. You know what? I do feel something. The same something, I always feel. Lonely, and pissed at myself for allowing this to happen.

"So, you missed this?"

Dan is unzipping his shorts as I stare rather blankly at him. Honestly, no, I did not miss his dick, but I missed him. I've been missing my good friend who's horrible at relationships. But now is not the time for a serious talk, so I drop to my knees and take him into my mouth.

He's moaning and running his fingers through my hair and I'm feeling depressed. This isn't even on a subconscious level. I truly just am not into this. Maybe this is the end. The end that should have arrived years ago for us. Perhaps people do get to a point when it's just over. Or perhaps I am allowing myself to feel nothing because I know my feelings won't be returned. What I do know is that I am tired of this same set of thoughts running through my mind every time I am with him. Dear God please help me love myself more.

He's now hard and ready to enter me but before he does, he asks. "Did you clean your booty?"

"Yes, but please don't start there."

"Why not?"

"Because I want to feel you inside me first."

"I will be inside you."

"You know what I mean."

"Yeah, I know, and I'm going to give it to you in every one of your holes."

I really hope I meet Shemar Moore this year and we fall madly in love. My thoughts are interrupted by Dan. He's gone a little limp. I can tell he's noticed my lack of enthusiasm and it's caused his arousal to tank. I suck some more and he's now ready.

Five years and the same position. Doggy style. Nothing new about this, except for the hotel room. He gives me a few whacks on the ass, calls my name, pulls my hair, and then turns me over to suck some more. I take him in again, this time with a sense of desperation. I'm sucking his dick as though I'm wildly in love with it – not him, but his dick. I take a deep breath and allow all of him into the depths of my throat. I'm good at this, and he loves it. I pull back and swirl my tongue around his tip and slightly inhale. This always makes him quiver. Then, I inhale and take in his hardness to the back of my throat once again.

"Ava, you're such a bad girl. Are you my naughty girl?"

I mumble out an "um-hum" as he is deep in my throat. I feel the need get some pleasure tonight, so I think I'm going to masturbate while I'm deep throating him. I'm on my side with my head on his chest, so it's easy to spread my legs and give myself some loving. Must be this device still stuck in right brain mode, as I've never done this before – never been so bold as to pleasure myself while giving head.

"Damn, that shit is sexy girl! I love watching you suck me and play with yourself."

My masturbation and head have gotten Dan hard again, and this time I'm positioned in doggy-style, but he's entering my ass. I wince with pain as he forces himself inside me. I fucking hate this shit, but I let out a few moans to fake the pleasure he wants me to feel.

More calling my name and slapping my ass and then Dan collapses. He seems satisfied. We curl up in the bed and spoon. I close my eyes thinking we are both drifting off to sleep.

"Do you think you're going to like it out there?"

"I already do. It's gorgeous and the fellowship so far is quite liberal. I can research whatever I want and the other fellows I met are great. So, how's life on the Hill and the real estate market?"

"About over for the Hill. One more week to go and I've signed on with a broker so I'm moving forward with my plans.

"Wow, I wish I could do something like that."

"You can, Ava. This conversation is déjà vu. We've talked about this before."

"I guess but…"

"But nothing. You own a business. You've made that work. For the love of God, why do you do this?"

"Do what?"

"Sell yourself so short?"

"I'm not sure, but you are truly an inspiration."

Dan is truly an ass, but I have to give it to him he does go for what he wants, and he always excels. That's probably why he just fucked me in the ass, and I hated it – he wanted it and got what he wanted as always.

"Whatever, get off your ass and do whatever it is you want to do and be your own damn inspiration."

"Okay, gee, what's with the meanness."

"Sorry but, Ava, you are one of the smartest people I know, and it floors me that you can't see how great you are."

"If I'm so great, why is it all you want from me is to fuck me?"

"Whoa, where the fuck did that come from? Ava, I've told you a hundred times it's me, not you, and this is my deal. I don't want a relationship. I just want a fuck buddy."

"Yeah, you have."

"So, let's not go there, and let's enjoy this night, okay?"

I don't think most fuck buddies spend the night and spoon and have motivational chats, but maybe they do. How would I know? This is my first fuck buddy experience. And for five years now, it looks like every other committed relationship I've been in before.

"Okay."

We curl up and Dan quickly drifts off to sleep.

I need to do the same, as my start time is incredibly early tomorrow. I'm entangled in my thoughts. Hopefully, I will drift off soon.

5

Trust

I've survived my first day of orientation and I'm ready to hang out with Dan. I know this is the worst relationship for me, but it's something, and it makes being 3,000 miles away from everyone and everything I know less lonely.

Today, I'm wearing a cute turquoise and paisley halter dress with beige wedge sandals. Maybe if I dress more girly with the heels Dan will take more of an interest.

I hear the knock on the door, and I walk across the room to open it. As I do I see he's holding a bottle of wine and a big smile.

"I forgot to bring this last night."

"Nice. Let me get some glasses."

I open the cabinet over the sink and pull out two wine glasses. Dan is opening the bottle with the opener he found in the nearby drawer. As he pours the wine, I give him a half-smile.

"So how was your day? Orientation going well?"

"Yeah, great. A lot of stuff I already know. Briefings from all the offices in the building but it's good for those folks who haven't work at the HAF (Headquarters Air Force) before."

"Man, that shit has got to be boring as hell for you."

"It is, but tomorrow we take a trip to the White House Executive building!"

"That should be cool."

"Oh, yeah, no big deal to the Senator's chief of staff, right?"

"Right."

Dan is smiling and is amused by my excitement. I've not shared with him my secret desire to be Secretary of State and follow in the path of Susan Rice by becoming the National Security Advisor. Never mind our career paths are polar opposites and never mind this would be going down a path that I have dreamed up for myself to continue to fit into the imagine everyone has for me. Forbid I tell everyone especially my parents that I want to complete this fellowship, work off the five years I will owe for the Air Force paying for the fellowship and then set myself free to finally live my life as a writer.

"This is good." I lift my glass and swirl the wine around as I smile at him.

"Thanks, I know you love red."

"Sure."

I should really let him know that I don't. I always get the most brain throbbing headaches when I drink red wine. There has got to be a reason I am so accommodating to him – to everyone. I really need to rethink skipping therapy for the next year.

"So, what's on TV?"

"I don't know."

I hand him the remote and he starts flipping through the channels.

We are sitting on the couch, curled up and drinking our wine. This feels so right. Why in the world can't this man just love me? Better question, why can't he want what I want? I know he loves me, or rather he's said he cares for me, so why can't I get the committed relationship from him?

Dan has landed on *Bad Boys II* and is immediately turning up the volume. It's the scene where all the dead bodies are falling out of the van.

He leans over and gives me a kiss on the forehead and takes a sip of his wine. He loves me, I just know he does. Maybe I should tell him exactly why I know this to be true.

The movie ends with me half asleep, and my head on Dan's shoulder.

"Wake up, sleepyhead."

As I open my eyes, I see Dan's penis. He has unzipped his pants and is ready for sex. Dear Lord, why? I'm so sleepy, but I know I have to have sex with him. He wants it, and it's only fair since he came over a second day. I don't hate having sex with Dan, I just wish we could do it in a position other than doggy style. We make our way to the bed and sucking begins. I am surprised as Dan positions me into sixty-nine so he can lick and suck on me down there, as well. I have to hand it to him; the man can give some great head. I am so aroused and feeling so ready for this that I move on top of him. He is surprised but goes with the flow. As I am riding him, I am so turned on and I can tell he's loving it too. We are so close, skin on skin, our lips close to formulating a kiss. I lean in closer, and he obliges. The connection between us brings me closer to a climax, and as I do, our eyes lock. His passionate gaze is turning hard. He closes his eyes, and his movement stops. It must be time for me to suck some more. I quickly move to take him into my mouth, but he rolls over on his side.

I'm stunned and at a loss for words, but I manage to get out, "Are you okay?"

"No, fuck, Ava, I'm not. Why are you being so selfish?"

"Selfish?"

"Can't you let me have my pleasure as well?"

"I thought you were, you looked like you were."

"I'm supposed to cum first."

"So, I am not allowed to cum, to enjoy myself?"

"No, not at my expense. We make love and I get my pleasure and then you get yours."

Did he just say, "make love"? He's never, ever used this phrase before.

"I'm confused."

"Don't play innocent with me."

Dan is getting out of the bed and looking for his clothes. Is he leaving?

"What are you doing?"

"I'm going home. I can't trust you, Ava."

"What?"

"I can't trust you. Good luck with your fellowship."

I'm in complete shock as I watch him get dressed.

"Please, don't go. Not like this. I don't know the next time we'll see each other after this week."

"That's not my fucking problem!"

"Please lower your voice. I am on this floor with other fellows. Please don't embarrass me like this."

"No worries. I'm out."

I'm sitting on the bed, naked and crying. I'm not sure how we got here, but then again, I do. It's all too much to process right now.

Dan is walking towards me. He looks furious. He bends over and attempts to kiss me on my lips, but I turn my head.

"Just leave."

I say as I choke on my words.

He turns and heads out the door.

I am so fucking confused right now. Is he seriously leaving? And what does he mean he can't trust me? He's said on more than one occasion I am the only person he can trust.

I should have let him me fuck me doggy style. We were too intimate for him. I think, no, I *know* he loves me, and this big ass wall he keeps up has crumbled a little just now, all because we were fucking face-to-face.

I leap out of the bed to look for my phone.

"Hello?"

"Can you come back, please?"

"No."

"It's the middle of the night."

"Ava, I live ten minutes away. I'll be fine, but I can't be with you. I can't trust you."

"Please tell me what this means."

"You know."

"No, I do not. Help me understand."

"I just can't trust you."

"But…"

"I'm hanging up now. I'm letting you know so you won't think I'm being rude and hanging up on you. Enjoy the Executive Building tomorrow and have a good rest of the week. Goodbye."

I thought the worst part of this trip was locking the girls and myself out of our apartment right before heading to the airport on Sunday, but clearly this beats that by a longshot.

Bewildered and dismayed, I locate my pajamas, get dressed, and crawl back into bed. I cry for a while and slowly begin to feel myself fall asleep.

6

Hello, Shawshank

This week has been hell after the incident with Dan the other night, but I have managed to keep a smile on my face and suffer through this orientation. Today, we were given an extra-long lunch break so I'm heading over to say hello to my Shawshank crew.

I check my phone as I wait for the train at the Crystal City Metro. Nothing from Dan. I am still in disbelief. We've had falling outs before, including my questioning our exclusivity just a couple of months ago which he took offense to and stop speaking to me for a while. And, over the years, one of us can find a way to push the other's buttons to the point of a brief separation but the "I don't trust you" thing? Where did that come from? Especially when he's said so many times that I'm the only one he can trust. And "make love"? We fuck, plain and simple. All these mixed messages are too much to process when I'm surrounded by a sea of Air Force Fellows and endless hours of briefings and tours.

The train arrives and I enter. It's midday so it's not crowed, but I opt not to sit. The Pentagon is just two stops away and honestly, I feel if I sit down, I might not get up. I could sit on this blue line train and ride it all the way to Largo and back and still not be ready to face the remainder of this week.

As the train enters the Pentagon Metro and stops, I shake my head and out of nowhere I reach down to touch my wrist. Man, I could use this device right now. Left brain would take away all these feelings and shit. I've got one more day here before I fly back to California, and I haven't reached out to Monique. Maybe I'll give her a call tonight, though I have no idea how long it would take her to fix this thing. I should at least tell her it's broken. She's going to kick my ass when she finds out it's been broken for several months now. Anyway, pull it together, Ava, and put on your "Another great Air Force day" Stepford Wife smile.

As the escalator ascends to the street level, I feel a since of relief. This is only a visit, not the working sentence I had been serving since 2007. I guess you can say I am on parole, and I am here visiting my former inmates.

I pull out my badge, beaming. Two of my favorite Pentagon Police Officers are checking badges this afternoon.

"Hey, y'all!"

"Hey yourself! Haven't seen you in a few weeks."

"I'm out in Santa Monica for a fellowship for the next year."

"Well, now that's nice!"

"Just back for a quick trip?"

"Yeah, then it's back to the beach! See y'all later!"

"Oh, she got to rub that part in!"

"Yeah, she do! You go girl!"

I give them a wink and smile as I approach the doors to Shawshank.

I make my way inside and head to my office. I've only been gone two weeks, yet it feels somewhat foreign being in here today. I'm sure it's because I know I don't have to stay. There are no taskers for me to work and Marcy, my OSD Policy nemeses, will not be threating me with the wheels up bullshit she loves. I am not sure if she ever realized

I didn't give a shit about when the SecDef was wheels up. I am a GS-14 who doesn't control shit, and if the Air Force is last on a coordination effort that the SecDef needs prior to some meeting because the Air Force Secretary or Chief have issues with our response, I have little control over this, nor does my Col or two- or three-star generals for that matter. All we can do is answer their questions until they are satisfied and sign off on the package.

I make it just inside my office and run smack into Col Baker.

"Ava! Long time no see! Oh wait, short time no see, right? Ha, yep, that one was funny."

"Sure, Sir. How are you?"

"Same thing different day."

"Groundhog Day."

"What? Like the movie? Okay, yeah sure! So, how's the L.A. area? Are you settled in?"

"It's great, and yes. I'm back this week for the orientation."

"Yeah, I had to do that when I went to Air War College. It's a good way to network. You'll spend the year with just a handful of Air Force folks at Big Brains, but this week you'll meet all the Fellows from the various programs."

"Yes, I've met quite a few this week, but I'm not that interested in networking."

"Really, why not?"

"None of this matters."

"Hum, well, now, I wouldn't say that too loud or someone will wonder why they're paying for you to be out there for a year."

"I'm wondering the same thing, Sir, but I will say I'm paying for me to be out there."

"How's that?"

"I've been paying taxes for twenty years, so I've more than paid for my per diem and the lodging I've been so graciously given."

"Point taken."

"Ava, you know, before you left you were starting to act a little strange. I thought the fellowship would help you reset, and I'm still certain it's what you need. You are one of our best, and I know this place has burnt you out. Take this year and enjoy. Go learn crap that has nothing to do with the Air Force. Hell, Big Brains has their hands in everything from medical research to education. Detach from all things Air Force. Trust me, it will all be here when you return. And enjoy the damn beach!"

"Thanks for the advice, Sir. I will do that, with exception of my research paper. It's on Synchronization of Security Cooperation efforts across the Defense Department."

"Nice!"

"Ava!"

Al is smiling and waving at me as he rounds the corner.

"Thought I heard your voice! Welcome back!"

"Thanks, just wanted to pop in and say hi and see if you needed anything."

"Hi, and nope. You did a fantastic job of getting everyone up to speed on your projects and you left everything nicely organized on the share drive, so we're good."

Col. Baker checks his watch.

"Gotta go! Coffee meeting in five. Good to see you, Ava."

"Good to see you, Sir."

"Well, Al, I'd better head back before my lunch break is over."

"Good seeing you, Ava, take care!"

"You too!"

I turn to leave and smile. I know I won't be returning to this office after the fellowship. I signed a mobility agreement, but I know I'll end up somewhere back in the bowels of Shawshank. As I pointed out to Mandy the other day, the best always find their way here. And not be vain, but I am one of the best. The sad part is I've already been here for eight years so returning will be nothing more than status quo, only I am certain I will get a promotion after this fellowship as well. I will finally achieve the grade of GS-15, something had I stayed in Oklahoma would have occurred years ago. I was slated to replace my boss, who was moving on to a different job. My leadership even created a new position to ensure I would easily slide in as his replacement. But, to everyone's surprise, I left. Running away from a broken heart and into a decade-long sentence as a GS-14. I knew it would be harder to get promoted once relocating to the Pentagon, but I didn't care. I needed to leave. I needed the fresh start, much like this year in Santa Monica is offering me – only instead a fresh start, it's more like a break from crazy. Crazy Shawshank and crazy ass Dan.

As I exit Shawshank and head to the Metro, I check my phone for the time and see I won't be late for the afternoon session. I will say it felt good being in the building for a brief time. I know I hate it there, but after all these years, it's become my reality, my crazy extended family. There's comfort in the crazy.

7

Going Back to Cali

Is it only in the movies where men chase after the women they love? Or is it that no man has ever loved me, so I have never been chased?

Orientation is over, and I am thankful to board this plane and get the hell away from this painful metropolis. Dan is known for picking ridiculous fights and giving me the silent treatment in the past, and every time it occurs it's because he feels we are getting too close. He never says this, but I know that's what it is. But this time, he's upset over the trust thing. That just hurt on a level I cannot describe – and to do it while I am away for a year, and to leave without saying goodbye? What the hell?

I'm hurt and broken, drained, and confused. This week has done it all to me, and yet I still love him. I still want him. A man who clearly has been hurt in a previous relationship and broken from childhood by his mother. I'm in love with a man who told me five years ago he didn't want to be in a relationship, yet here I am. Maya Angelou said when people tell you who they are, or show you who they are, believe them. I know this, but I fell in love with him anyway. Steve Harvey talks about it in his second book *Straight Talk No Chaser*. There are men who honestly do not want to be in a relationship.

I think it's my fear of being alone, or something. Whatever it is, it must die. I'm sitting on this plane texting Dan, telling him about my impressive experience at the Executive Building and stroking his ego about how cool it is that he's been able to go there whenever he wants. I just need a reply. I just need to keep hanging on. I need to have something in my life, something to hold on to as mine. For now, he's that something. It's a shame it can't be me.

I hit send.

My text to Dan reads:

I'm about to fly back to CA. The Executive Building was amazing! You are truly lucky to have had such great experiences as one of the people on The Hill. The fact that you can just walk into the building, the fact that you know these people is unbelievable to me!

I am surprised by his quick reply:

Yep, it's been great can't wait for the next new thing. Have a safe trip!

I want to reply but decide against it, as I have nothing worthwhile to say. Getting his response makes me feel good and makes me feel like I still have something to hold on to.

It's been a few weeks and my sadness over the Dan incident has faded. It always does, yet I never find enough strength to just walk away from it completely. Something is better than nothing, they say, but they are probably talking about things like money. One dollar is better than nothing, but a frustrated fuck buddy situation shouldn't be better than being alone and having a sense of self-worth. Again, why do I know this and yet do nothing?

Facebook, August 8, 2015

Happy Birthday Cleo 🎈🎈🎉🎈🎈 *Today my little girl is 11!!! My how time flies!*

Facebook, August 22, 2015

This morning I ran a total of 7 miles from Santa Monica to Pacific Palisades and back!

While there are others who can run faster and longer distances I am proud of myself because I haven't run in a while! My endorphins were kicking in as I was running to the Empire soundtrack mixed in with a little T.I. and the theme from Rocky 😊

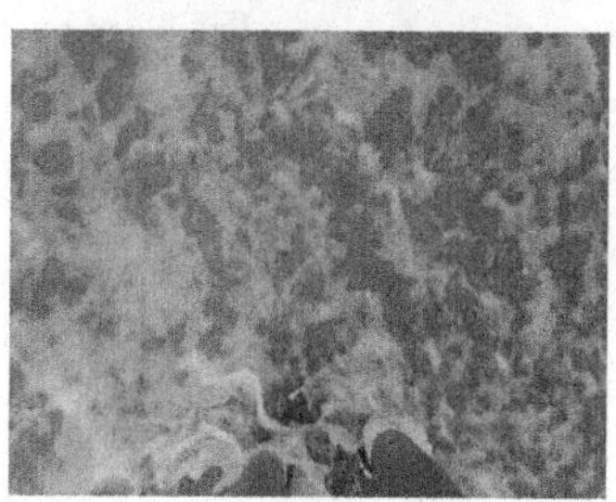

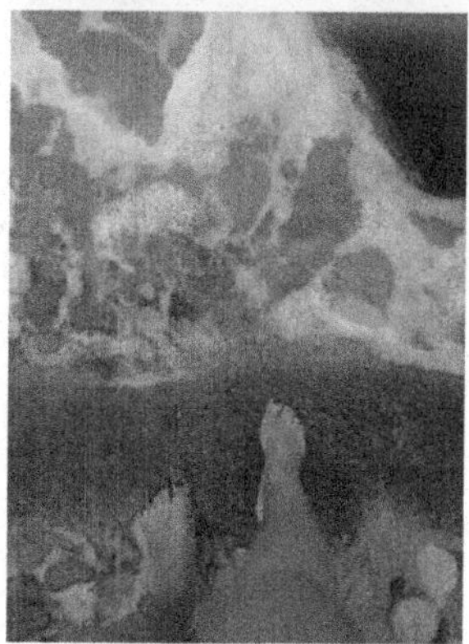

I also shared this with Dan via text but all I got in return was a good for you, Ava. He's pulling away. The "I don't trust you and am leaving you naked in a hotel bed crying" is his best performance to date. I really regret getting on top of him during sex that last night. I knew that was too intimate for him. Sure, we've done it before, especially after I got this device and fucked him in right brain mode. He loved my aggression. But that was the difference! Damn it, Ava! You weren't fucking aggressive, you were passionate. You weren't just on top bouncing around or riding him like some jockey, you were stroking him with your body. You were kissing him with love and affection. Yes, he was enjoying it, but as soon as he got a hold of his senses, he withdrew his passion and put that damn wall back up. Had I just gone with the status quo, or even my new right brain dominatrix role, we'd be good right now. Damn, this is all my fault! But I still want more than this bizarre friends with benefits shit because, truthfully, we act like so much more. Or maybe we don't. Maybe I've never had a decent loving committed relationship so to me this is more than friends with benefits but to the average person it's clearly a fuck buddy arrangement. Dan says it's just how he is when he's in a sexual relationship with someone. He says he's caring and affectionate, but it means nothing. I've told him on more than one occasion that he's better off fucking and leaving. This way there's no confusion, but he's never done that, and it's led me to believe he has more feelings for me than he lets on. Or maybe it's because I've heard him on two different occasions say he loves me when he was talking in his sleep.

"Ava, you know I'm in love with you, but I am too fucked up to be with you like that. You deserve better."

This was the first time. The second time he said, *"Ava, I will always love you."*

I've never bothered to tell him this as that would only send him completely over the edge. So, I live with truth while he perpetuates this lie. In either case, nothing has gotten better since my return to Santa Monica. I should just accept the end of this weirdness and move on with my life. It doesn't matter if he loves me, he clearly doesn't plan to do shit about it.

In either case I kicked butt today! And it is needed as I have been making far too many trips to the vending machine at work each day. I am not sure what this candy bar obsession is about but at least I'm exercising and burning off the calories.

Facebook, September 7, 2015
Best Labor Day ever!!! Rented a cute little beach cruiser today and biked 10.5 miles with a nice stop in Venice.

8

DMV…Again

Facebook, September 16, 2015
Heading to the Congressional Black Caucus' Annual Legislative
Conference - time to get my knowledge and networking on!

I sent Dan an email a couple of weeks ago letting him know I would be in town, but he didn't seem to care. His response was indifferent. Yesterday, he sent me an email telling me he thought we should just be friends. He thought I was looking for more out of our relationship than he was willing to give. Of course, I wrote him back and cussed him out. I told him I was fine with our fuck buddy situation, but I know he knows I'm lying. He then replied the sex was not satisfying for him, and that cut about as deep as the "I don't trust you" bullshit from July. He doesn't want me, and yet I'm holding on for dear life like he's my ticket to Heaven. I blame my parents for this, for feeling desperate for someone to love me. Of course, after years of therapy I know that's some bullshit too. I have to own my shit so it's me. I am the one who's to blame.

I'm changing planes in Dallas and have an hour layover. I can't shake the feeling I need to make a call. I want to call the lady I met in D.C. a few months ago before coming out to California. I met her when Sheryl asked me to join her at the Integrative Healing Center (IHC) to discuss the benefits of body cleansing. During our visit, Amy gave us a great deal of information on cleansing as well other areas she specializes in. She does these energy readings and healings, or something like that. I've never heard of such a thing, but she noted something about chakras, and I do recall a Dr. Oz episode on the subject. In either case, something is telling me I need to see her.

I find my way to my gate and pull out my phone. I look up an old email from Amy where she'd sent additional information on the cleansing and locate her cell phone number. I send her a text:

Hello this is Ava McClure. We met in April at IHC. I was wondering if you had any free time this week for an energy session. I will be in town until Thursday. Thanks.

I put my phone away and begin my search for coffee. As I'm standing in line waiting to order, my phone rings – it's Amy.

"Hello?"

"Hi, Ava, this is Amy."

"Hi, Amy, how are you. Thanks for calling back so quickly."

"My pleasure. You would like to come in for an energy reading is that correct?"

"Yes, I know this is last minute but if there is any way you can fit me in, I'd be greatly appreciative."

"Oh, no problem at all. I have some availability tomorrow at noon."

"Perfect! Thanks!"

"Do you need the address?"

"Um, no I have it so I'm good to go."

"Wonderful. I look forward to seeing you tomorrow."

"Likewise, and thanks again."

I don't know why in the hell I'm asking for an energy session. What I know is her description of the session, of the Chakra stuff, sounded so peaceful. It had an unspoken promise of clarity, and the freedom from bullshit that I am so desperately needing.

9

Reiki?

I've just check into the hotel. I'm impressed with its 1920s charm. I'm laughing to myself because if it were the 1920s, I wouldn't be allowed to stay here but, just the same, it's historically chic and right across from the Convention Center where the conference is located.

I'm extremely excited about this week. I've even decided to go the Black Party and brought with me an ultra-sexy, too-tight dress. I recall trying it on and telling the sales lady it was a little sung in the hips, to the point that it was making those creases in the middle of the dress. She said it was perfect and this is how they did it on the West Coast. I told her I was going to wear it on the East Coast to a party that would be flooded with the nation's political elite, and she said, "Then wear it this way and show those D.C. snobs how to dress!"

I felt briefly empowered at this thought, but then asked for the tailor. Once she arrived, she had me try on a dress a size larger and I could see the sales lady's point. Why not show off God's gift – my body? I purchased the size four. Thinking about it some more, I am convinced the two of them were in cahoots. I am sure they thought they were doing me a favor, and heck, I might just turn a few heads at the party!

I am also debating if I should let Dan know I'm in town, as I am just a block from his place. I know the answer is no, but I must let the thought cross my mind. It's late and I have an early start, so I'm going to lay out my suit for tomorrow and head to bed.

I'm feeling melancholy, sitting in the coffee shop across from the Convention Center eating breakfast. I've flown back across the country to attend a conference that I didn't make any effort to attend when I lived here for eight years. I've convinced myself I am here for Representative's Bass' Africa Summit, and to meet with some folks back in the Pentagon for my research paper, but I know in my heart I was hoping to connect with Dan. I can't believe I've left my babies for this. Thinking more about it, I'm here on my own dime, so why am I going to make time to go to Shawshank?

I make my way across the street and find my way to the registration. I pick up my badge. I'm registered as a business owner, "Lil Bits Dog Care," my semi-defunct dog walking and pet sitting business. I am sure I'll get back into the swing of this entrepreneurship thing once I'm back here for good, but for now it's all about the beach and my soon-to-be run-in with Shemar Moore (a girl is still hoping) while I'm out West.

Just wrapped up the Town Hall meeting and I'm feeling motivated. Black Lives Matter!

Facebook, September 17, 2015
Attended the Annual Legislative Conference's National Town Hall on
Black Lives Matter. You can follow on Twitter #LJFA

It's now time to hop on the Metro and head to my appointment with Amy. The clinic is in the Friendship Heights area of D.C. I love this area as it is D.C.'s version of Rodeo Drive – or at least that's how I see it. Wisconsin Avenue is lined with designer stores, from Tiffany to Dior to Louis Vuitton. I imagine becoming so successful with my writings and dog walking business that I'll someday stroll down this street and buy whatever I want. Today, I am here for an energy reading, or healing, or something to that effect. I feel in my bones that I need to be here.

I'm excited and not really that nervous. I just know I need fixing and I am hopeful this will do the trick. The way Amy described the process seems very tranquil, lying down while energy flows into her and then to me, checking each of my chakras while providing healing energy. I am sure there is more to it, but that's what I remember from our conversation a few months ago.

Entering the lobby, I see Amy waiting for me. She has the most peaceful look about her. She's dressed in a very loose-fitting light blue dress and her brunette hair is pulled back in a bun. She appears to be in her fifties, but I can't tell. She's dressed so nondescript she seems ageless.

"Ava, so nice to see you."

"It's nice to see you too."

"Are you ready to get started?"

"Sure."

This is pleasant. Most medical establishments require a wait time and a load of paperwork to be filled out, but I'm guessing not here, because she is motioning for me to follow her to the back. As we walk down the hall I am struck by the simplicity of the space – mint green walls with no decorations. Each room we pass has a small amount of equipment that I am unable to identify, or a couple of chairs and what appears to be a massage table. I was just here in April, but, being with Sheryl, I guess I wasn't attentive to the décor, or the contents of the rooms. As we turn the corner, Amy opens a door for me to enter. This room is also quite simple- beige walls, two folding chairs and a massage table. I take a seat, place my purse on the floor, and Amy sits across from me.

"You look lovely today," she says.

"Thanks, I just came from a conference."

I am dressed in a black fitted suit with a pale pink blouse. I wouldn't say I look lovely as much as I look like any other ordinary government or businessperson roaming around the District today.

"You are here for an energy reading, correct?"

"Yes, that is correct. Though I'm not really sure what it entails."

Amy explains the process as she glances at the massage table next to me. She notes something about Reiki, and source energy flowing through me, and healing any current issues. She asks if I know what chakras are and I stumble through my recollection from Dr. Oz that there are seven energy wheels in our body that impact our mind, body, and spirit. She seems pleased with my response.

"Well, let's start with what's going on in your life. Is there something in particular you are concerned about?"

"Yes, there is. My inability to move on from a relationship that is not working for me."

"Oh?"

"Yes, I've been in therapy for years now, but I can't seem to walk away. There is nothing about this relationship that is good for me, but I have such low self-esteem that I keep holding on anyway."

"Well, that's impressive you already know what the issue is."

"I think it's all the therapy. I've talked about it for years, but if I know what it is then why can't I let it go?"

"Let's start with your family. Can you tell me about them?"

"Sure, my parents are still married, and I have an older sister. I've never felt like I really belonged, though, as they have spent all my life doting on my sister. I have always tried to fit in, but I'm just so different from them."

I have this statement wrapped up with a bow. If nothing else, I got this message loud and clear from my sessions with Dr. Smith.

"So, you have been seeking their love and attention?"

"Oh, yes, most definitely."

Amy is looking at me with the most loving expression and I'm not sure why, but I feel this shift in me as we are talking. It's hard to describe, but a warm sensation seems to be filling my body. Maybe it's just my nerves.

"And this relationship?"

"This relationship is me looking for love from someone who doesn't want to give it. I know this. I think I'm so wired to seek love from those who are not wanting to love me that I attract these types of men into my life. I want to do better, but I just don't know how to make the change."

"Have you heard of Affect Bridge hypnosis?"

"No, I have not."

"It's a powerful technique I think you would benefit greatly from. It involves reliving various aspects of your childhood through hypnotherapy and working through the issues that have resulted in who you are today, and the choices you make. It's a lengthy process and we wouldn't have time today, but I do have some time tomorrow if you are interested?

"Yes, I would. That sounds amazing."

Did I just agree to be hypnotized?

"Great, so for today let's do an energy reading and healing."

"Okay."

Amy instructs me to remove my shoes and lay on the table. I'm excited to see how this will go.

My eyes are closed and there's that heat again. I feel it moving up my body. After what seems like an hour of silence, she asks in a voice just above a whisper, "How are you with communicating?"

"Not the best," I whisper back.

"Have you noticed any issues with your throat lately?"

"Yes, I've have. About a week ago, I awoke from my sleep choking. It was rather strange and lately I keep eating candy bars at work. I eat them in under ten seconds and it's like I'm stuffing my throat with them."

"Well, that explains why you have a blocked throat chakra."

"Oh," I say with my eyes still closed.

I'm not sure what else to say.

"We will send loving energy and light to heal it."

"Okay," I whisper.

I can sense her standing over me, but the energy feels stronger than her physical presence. It's as if there is more than Amy in the room – the energy of many beings not just one. If I didn't know any better I would think there were hundreds of people standing around me but that's absurd! I'm transformed, but into what I can't really say. I'm heavy and light all at the same time. It's as if I am both glued to this massage table and floating at the same time, and this intense flow circulating around and through my body is relaxing me. It feels intoxicating. I feel a sense of heat and sometimes it is followed with a coolness. There are parts of my body that are tingling; my fingers they are tingly and feel as though electricity is pulsating in my fingertips and now this same feeling has reached my throat where she said she's sending love and energy. These electric sensations continue down my body and the room feels as if more people have joined us. I want to open my eyes to see. I know that's silly as it's only the two of us yet can't help but feel the presence of so many more.

I hear Amy speaking. I believe she's praying, but I'm not sure. She's now lifting my right hand and stroking it. She moves to my left hand and does the same. I feel her lift my right foot and begin to move it in a circular motion.

"Let go," she whispers.

"Okay," I whisper back, but I can feel how tense my foot is. No matter how much I try to relax, I can't stop moving my leg in the circular motion.

"You have to try and let go. You don't have to always be in control. You have to learn to trust God."

"Okay," I whisper again as she lowers my leg.

She is now lifting my left foot, and here we go again.

"What is this you are holding on to?"

"I don't know," I say in a slightly louder voice.

I'm still very peaceful lying on this table, but my awareness is now heightened by my inability to do something as simple as relaxing my foot and letting someone move it. What is this? Am I that uptight?

As she lowers my foot she notes, "You have some deep-rooted trust issues. This is something we can work on. Tomorrow's session should help."

"Okay," I say still barely over a whisper.

I truly do hope so as I can't continue on like this.

This thing I am experiencing at this moment is new, yet it seems to be awakening parts of my soul. How can this be so sudden? I haven't been on this table that long, and yet things are stirring inside me. I'm confused but feel good. I feel safe. She is now saying a blessing for me, and I'm in such a place of peace. I don't want this to end. Just as I have this thought, Amy instructs me off the table and on to a nearby chair. I move to sit up and slowly place my feet on the floor. I find my way to the chair and sit down. She proceeds to lift my arms by my elbows.

"Relax."

"I'm trying," I whisper with a slight chuckle. It's not that I find this funny, but it's my standard reaction when I'm nervous.

Amy says more words over me and tells me we are done. I open my eyes and look up at her. She is smiling ever so peacefully. I am way too relaxed.

"How do you feel?"

"Good, thank you."

"That's wonderful."

I'm expecting more or some type of instruction, but Amy is just smiling. I guess this is it.

"I'm looking forward to tomorrow."

"Me too. I'll walk you out."

"Thanks."

I slip my heels back on and grab my purse. Amy opens the door, and we walk in silence as we head to the front of the clinic. I'm still dazed as I pay for my service, I guess. I don't recognize this feeling. I think it is peace, but I don't think I've every experience it before. I hope it lasts forever.

The ride back on the Metro is quiet but, then again, it's only a little after 2 PM, so there are very few riders. I've only driven my car in California. I am not near a train stop, though there is a new stop in works just a few blocks from our apartment. Many are concerned that a stop right in Santa Monica will bring with it more crowds of an urban nature. I imagine that's true. I see it in Pentagon City, the folks from D.C. taking the Metro to the closest mall. Then there was the mass freak out over the Silver Line. The upper-middle class in the Tyson's Corner area were nervous about the expansion of the Metro. They had this belief that those from D.C. would venture further out and steal from the elite stores at Tyson's Corner. I recall watching the news stories on this panic. I remember thinking, "That's a long way to steal some shit, and I am not sure having a train that runs every seven or fourteen minutes is the best getaway strategy." Seems like if the security in the stores and around the mall were doing their job, they would catch these thieves, and after a few of these arrests the plot to rob Tyson's would fade. But what do I know? The whole thing was rooted in racism anyway.

It's too late to head back to the conference and tonight is the Black Party, so I think it's best if I swing by my favorite nail salon in Crystal City and get primped for my big night.

"Ava!"

I'm greeted by the salon owner as I enter.

"Hi, Sue!"

I love Sue, she is an expert in gel manicures and pedicures and is the only person I trust in the DMV to wax my eyebrows.

"I thought you were in California?"

"I am. I'm back for a conference. There's a party tonight and I was hoping you could work me in for a mani-pedi and brow wax,"

Looking around, I only see one other person in the salon. It's just 3 PM and I've made it in before the evening rush.

"Yes, of course." Sue walks over to start running water in one of the basins for my pedicure. I follow behind her, smiling at the other nail techs. This place has been my second home since my great Oklahoma Escape of 2007.

"So, how is it out there?"

"Wonderful! I love it and my fellowship is great."

"So, what happened to your boyfriend?"

I've always referred to Dan as my boyfriend to Sue, and to mostly everyone except my girlfriends. It's just easier this way though, whenever I do, I am overtaken with sadness because I know it's a lie.

"Oh, he's good."

Sue's phone rings and she answers. She begins speaking in Vietnamese, so I have no clue what's she's saying but she's laughing hysterically.

Hearing her voice in this foreign language allows me to zone out. I'm relaxed as she gives me my pedicure.

She wraps up her phone call as she finishes my pedicure. She is about to ask me something as I sit at her table for my manicure, but her phone rings again, and she is back to speaking Vietnamese. She stays on the phone for the duration of my manicure and only hangs up because she has to do my brows. As we walk to the back, she turns to me and says, "Sorry for all the phone calls."

"No worries," I say.

"So, what is this party tonight?"

"It's just a get-together with all the people from this conference."

Actually, I have no idea what this will be like. I have this vision of me walking into the club and turning a bunch of heads, having lively small talk with congresspeople, senators and maybe even a celebrity or two. I'm hoping for Roland Martin and Donna Brazile, for starters, but who knows who shows up for these things.

My brows are on fleek, or at least I think that's what people say. I'm feeling good and still very peaceful as I make my way back to the Crystal City Metro. It's now rush hour, so I am surrounded by more people, but I'm headed north, and most folks are going in the opposite direction, so it's still a very pleasant ride.

Exiting at Mt Vernon Square Metro, I'm feeling less like partying and more like walking. It's a nice day and I'm not really in the mood for a crowd of people, though it would be a shame to let my uber expensive new dress go to waste. Truthfully I am never in the mood for crowds, I was just trying to push myself to do something new.

Back in my room, I'm standing in the bathroom staring at myself in the mirror. I look sexy as hell in this dress! The sales lady and the tailor were right, tight is the way to go!

Facebook, September 17, 2015
When you know you're looking good but you're rolling solo and trying to take a full-length selfie with unbelievably bad bathroom lighting 😊 *Normally I wouldn't share but this is just too funny not to!*

Well, at least I showed off my look to the few Facebook friends I have. Now I can take this dress off and change into some jeans. I've known since I started getting dressed an hour ago that I wasn't going to the party, but somewhere in my mind I held on to some small hope that if I went through the motions, I would convince myself to go. It didn't work. It never does. I do it when I want to attend a new church. I get up, get dressed, grab my bible, drive to the church, and then drive off. I've done it for dates. I've gotten dressed, headed to the coffee shop, and then turned around about fifty feet out and gone home. I'm sure this has some deep-rooted issue behind it, but I never brought it up with Dr. Smith. In either case, I just feel like walking around D.C. and that's what I'm going to do this evening.

The elevator in this hotel is tiny. I get historic preservation, however a larger elevator would have been a nice upgrade, though I'm guessing there's building codes or something that would make this impossible. This wouldn't even be an issue if I were not stuck in this old-fashioned box with a very hands-on couple. I am all for PDA, but really, if they move one inch it will be my ass he's groping.

We finally reach the lobby and I hurry out. I take a moment to walk over to the bar in the hotel. It's small and loud. There's a band in the corner warming up for the night. Maybe I'll treat myself to a drink after my walk. Turning to walk out of the hotel, I see evening has turned to night. This should make for a peaceful outing, as we are now past rush hour.

I head east, or I think it's east. I'm walking down Massachusetts Avenue with the slowest of strides. I'm not the best with directions. I'm walking and soaking everything in. It's funny that I've lived in the DMV all these years and never really looked around, never taken in everything that's going on. Normally, I am with one or more of my girlfriends and we are enthralled in conversation, so seeing the church on the corner hosting a fish fry and noticing just how many homeless people there are all around me, is quite a revelation. I take a right on 9th St NW and make my way to New York Avenue. As I do, I see a familiar restaurant on the right. I recall eating there one evening a couple of years ago with Jamie. She is great at finding all the new hot spots in the District, and this place is definitely on the list. It's a Louisiana-themed restaurant and the food was amazing. I'm laughing to myself as I remember Jamie announcing she was eating as Jesus would eat, and therefore most of the items on the menu were off-limits. I just smiled at her and ordered my meal. Why in the world would she suggest a southern-styled seafood place if she were going to eat like Jesus? But that's Jamie.

I do miss my friends, though they wouldn't guess it, as I didn't bother to tell any of them I was back in town this week, or the week of the orientation. It's hard to explain, but I like the feeling of isolation right now. It's not a sad, poor Ava thing, it's just a peaceful enjoyment of me time. Getting away from this area has allowed me to do it and not look like an ass. Maybe they still think I am an ass, as moving across the country shouldn't end communication. I guess I'm just selfish right now and I'm okay with that. I don't have any guilt about it.

I've now wandered into Chinatown, and I see a large crowd entering the Verizon Center. I don't keep up with sports, so I am not sure if the Wizards are playing. Pre-game maybe? Hockey? Too early, I think. Perhaps a concert. I don't see any team jerseys, so I'm guessing it's not sports related.

Roaming aimlessly, I see I'm now on 14th St NW and heading straight for the club. There they are. The Annual Leadership Conference crew. The women in their sexy black dresses and the men in their sharp suits and me in my jeans and tennis shoes passing by. I'm trying to feel guilty about changing my mind and not attending, but it's not working. This walk is exactly what I need. Just walking with no relevant thoughts. Just a blissful late summer evening breeze, or maybe we're already into fall? I don't keep up with seasons.

A few more blocks and I am at the entrance of Dan's condo building. I wonder if I buzz him, would he be there? That would shock the shit out of him, but why do that? He doesn't want you, Ava, move on. So, I do. I walk a few more steps and find my way back on Massachusetts Avenue. I've walked a fairly big circle tonight, and now it's time for a drink. I find my way to the bar inside the hotel and climb up on to one of the bar stools. I hate being so short.

"Good evening, what can I get for you?"

"A glass of Chardonnay please."

"Sure thing."

The bartender, a tall bleach-blonde guy, hands me a menu and walks off to pour my wine. I am starving now that I think about it. I haven't eaten since this morning. I glance over the menu and decide on the beef nachos.

What a day: starting out at the conference and experiencing some unexplainable spiritual thing. What is it called exactly? Energy reading, cleansing, chakra balancing? Is it the same as that Reiki thing I've heard about? Amy did mention Reiki. I should look it up. I wonder how many people are so desperate for change that they call a stranger they've met once and subject themselves to what I did this afternoon in hopes of peace and happiness.

As I pull out my phone, the bartender sets my glass of wine on the bar. I place my order and begin my internet search. I don't get far. I just know it's changed me. It was hours ago, and I am still so mellow. I just want this feeling to last. I sip my wine and look around the bar. There are small groups of people laughing and drinking, and the band is in full swing. I hear it all but can't seem to really focus on any one thing. I'm tired and ready to go to bed. It's all I can do to eat some of my nachos before settling my bill and heading up to my room.

I'm undressing and running my bath water. I keep thinking about this hypnosis thing I so eagerly agreed to today. It's so not like me, but in this moment, in this time of my life, I am so hungry for something.

I've been in and out of therapy for years, and it's just not working for me. Maybe this alternative approach is more of my thing. Maybe it can move me to do better for myself. After all, it is spiritual, so there's a higher power involved. With therapy, there's just me – though I'm sure all my deeply religious girlfriends would tell me I'm never alone, and that the Holy Trinity is with me all the time. I don't disagree with this line of thinking, but I don't know, something about what happened earlier today is more aligned with my soul, and therapy seems more about my ego. But what do I know?

10

Hello Little Avas

My phone alarms at 7 AM and I hit snooze. It alarms repeatedly until finally I reset it for 9 AM. My interest in the conference has dwindled now with the thought of the hypnotherapy, and I have no desire to attend the morning sessions. The time for my session with Amy is during the Africa Summit, which was my main reason for attending the conference.

I'm now up and getting dressed. I am in jeans and a sheer floral blouse. No need for the suit today. This feels liberating. Big Brains is super casual and while it's only been two months I have quickly adapted. After years of racing around Shawshank in suits or dresses and four-inch heels, it is a welcomed change. So, ditching the suits while back in D.C. is all good with me.

I am really settling in nicely at Big Brains. Everyone there is pleasant, smart, and exceptionally relaxed. The Fellows have a "mandatory" lunch out of the office once a week. It's a time when we get to explore another great restaurant in Santa Monica. And, by we I mean the collective group – Army, Navy, Air Force, Marines, Coast Guard and Department of Homeland Security. Together there are 15 of us which makes for a fun outing each week. I've gotten to know each of them, and a few have made it to my close acquaintance circle meaning we hang out outside of the office and enjoy evenings and weekends together. A few of them are really into this alternative healing thing – essential oils, crystals, chakras. I think it's great that they are here this year as it gives me the opportunity to learn more about this world. I can't wait to tell them about my session with Amy though I am guessing they will have had many of these sessions and will be able to help me piece more of the experience together.

And I am so thankful this device is broken, and I didn't see Monique when I was here in July for the orientation. I know she would have fixed this damn thing and I would have been back to switching. I know this is true because I can't seem to concentrate on anything at Big Brains. They give you the freedom to explore any of their research areas and dig in as much or as little as you want, and I have dug into nothing. I have read a few publications from their health department and contributed a few thoughts to some research on a Security Cooperation project but that's it. I haven't really started on my research paper. It's the only requirement for the year and could easily be knocked out in about a month and yet it's September and I've only drafted an outline. And the research Big Brains is doing on Security Cooperation directly ties to my paper. I could be in lock step with that and get my name published with the report, but I'm not interested. I know had I the ability to switch to left brain I would be having a completely different experience at Big Brains but instead, I am arriving to work around 9 AM after swinging by and getting a vanilla latte at the coffee shop next door, ordering the most amazing breakfast items from their cook to order chef in the cafeteria, applying for every job I can find in the area and heading home around 4 PM all while dressed in jeans, a t-shirt and Chuck Taylors. I am fairly sure this is not what Col Baker had in mind when he said I needed a break from the beltway but it's what I am doing, and I am loving it!

Amy is waiting for me again today as I enter the clinic.

"Ava, good to see you."

"Good to see you too."

I'm waiting to get nervous but nope, nothing. We walk back to the same room we were in the yesterday, and I take a seat on the folding chair.

"So, how was the rest of your day?"

"It was good. Peaceful."

"That's great. I forgot to mention you should really try to avoid a lot of human interaction after a session, not a lot of talking."

"Oh, well that worked out. I did go to a nail salon, but the technician was so busy on the phone that we didn't talk like we normally do, and then I decided not to go to the conference party and instead I took a walk around D.C. and ate alone at the hotel bar."

"Well, good! The Universe has a way of taking care of us. Are you ready for today?"

"I am, yes."

Amy begins to explain the process of this therapy and I am intrigued. She's going to hypnotize me and then take me back through various stages of my childhood. As we go through each stage, I am to connect with the younger me. This is to help me heal from my past hurts and bring about a sense of self-love and empowerment. I am open to anything, and I am eager to get started.

"Yesterday, you mentioned wanting to move forward with your life."

"Yes, that is correct."

"Can you tell me what you want for yourself?"

"Oh, yes. I want to move forward and have a sense of self-love and respect for myself. I know I lack this and the way it impacts my decisions is incredible. I mostly want to do better at love, or rather, not allow myself to stay in bad relationships. Not that they are abusive, but they are neglectful, and I think that is like abuse."

"Yes, it is. You are very aware of your issue."

"Yes, I've had a lot of therapy, but I can't break away from these unhealthy choices."

"I see. Can you tell me more about your family? You mentioned not fitting in yesterday."

"Yes, there's four of us, my mom, dad and older sister. I would say I am the outcast of the family."

"Why is that?"

"I was unwanted. My parents have made it clear throughout my life that I was an accident. I know many children grow up hearing this and many turn out to be fine, but for me, I guess I internalized it more than others. Maybe it would be different had they said I was their happy accident? I've heard parents say that, but not mine. To make it clear, they have gone out of their way to dote on my sister and only provide the basic necessities for me. I think I've spent my life trying to get them to like me, or at least acknowledge that I'm an okay person. I do the same thing in my relationships."

"How does this make you feel?"

"Sad? I guess."

"It seems like you are analyzing your feelings verses actually feeling. You're holding back your emotions. Why?"

"I'm not sure. I wasn't aware that's what I do, but I guess I am suppressing my actual feelings." Wow, Dr. Smith never mentioned this, but then again, I think I'm supposed to be analyzing my feelings in therapy. This stuff is different, it's deeper, or something.

"I want you to tell me again how your family has treated you, and I want you to allow yourself to feel it."

I take a deep breath and begin the tell of my childhood. I can do this. I can let go and feel. As I spiral into the "woe is me" script, I begin to shake. It's uncontrollable and I begin to feel tears in my eyes. Amy hands me a tissue and I quickly wipe them away. I am embarrassed. I don't cry. And I most certainly don't cry in front of strangers. I never cried in therapy. What in the hell is happening? I'm sobbing uncontrollably sitting on this folding chair in the middle of Friendship Heights. The only thing I thought I'd be doing here is shopping after I had my finances in order. I'm sitting here bawling, and I'm supposed to be at the Africa Summit. What the hell?

I continue to tell of my hurt and pain and finally get to a stopping point with the tears.

"That was good."

Amy is smiling at me with the most loving look I've ever seen. I'm beginning to wonder if she's even real. How can someone this calming and insightful exist?

"I think we are ready for the hypnotherapy. Are you ready to begin?"

"Sure," I say, but hell if I know.

Between yesterday and this tear-fest, I am shook beyond any level of comprehension, but still, I don't hesitate to get up from the chair and make my way to the massage table.

Amy begins to walk me through the hypnosis. This is interesting. I am awake but relaxed. I am coherent and very much aware of myself and my surroundings. I wasn't expecting this.

"Tell me about your earliest memory of feeling abandoned."

"I was three and I was in my parents' bedroom. There was something on the top of the chest of drawers that I wanted, and I attempted to climb up to the top. I didn't get far before the chest fell, and I found myself underneath it. It was heavy and it hurt. I remember calling out to my parents, but no one came for a long time. I cried for a while longer, and then stopped and just laid there. Eventually they came, and my dad pulled the chest off me. No one said anything. He just pulled the chest up, and they went back to the living room to watch TV with my sister."

"How did that make you feel?"

"Scared, lonely."

"I want you to see that little Ava and tell her you are with her. Give her a hug. Let her know that she is not alone, and that you will always be there for her."

"Okay."

I visualize myself hugging my younger me and I begin to cry. Oh, little Ava, I'm so sorry, but I am here for you now. I love you and will always take care of you. I promise.

"Do you remember when you were five?"

"Yes."

"Do you have a memory you'd like to share?"

"Yes. It was my first day of kindergarten and my mom took me to school. We made it to the classroom door, and she said goodbye. When I looked around the room, I saw other kids with their parents, but my mom didn't stay. When I looked back, she was gone."

"How did this make you feel?"

"Confused and sad. Hurt, I would say."

"Can you comfort this little Ava too?"

"Yes."

My heart is aching with grief and love. I am feeling so full of compassion for this little girl, for me.

Oh, poor baby Ava, it's okay. I love you and I am here for you, always, always.

"Have you comforted this young Ava?"

"Yes, I have."

Amy continues to walk me through my childhood, progressing every couple of years. As she does, I meet thirteen-year-old Ava who was hurt and disappointed because her family thought nothing of her birthday. She was finally a teenager, and yet no one seemed to care. There was no fanfare, just a half-eaten cake that she had baked herself a couple days prior. I am watching her receive her gifts – an *Ebony* magazine from her sister, who knows she only reads *Fresh* and *Right On* because she is a huge New Edition fan. Her sister has purchased a magazine that she likes and plans to read herself, since she knows Ava won't be interested. She also receives some adjustable birthstone rings from her dad, but she doesn't wear jewelry except for over-the-top earrings – it was the '80s after all. Ava also received a picture of a unicorn, as well as a stuffed unicorn from her mom. Her mom was the most spot-on, but these were of interest to Ava a few years prior, and she's now outgrown them. Did no one in her family know her or care? I am seeing myself ask my sister to take a picture of me blowing out the candles on the cake. The three candles I placed on a half-eaten cake I baked. I have to turned it around to make it appear as though it was a whole cake, made just for my birthday. In this hypnotic state, I am right there feeling the sadness as though it's 1986 – only I am not feeling it *as* thirteen-year-old Ava, I am feeling it *for* her. I embrace her tightly and I don't want to let go. Is this where Ava started to harden, is this where the wall started to be built? It didn't start with her first bad breakup, it started here. It was being erected while she was trapped under that chest of drawers. It's been building all her life.

How could she feel anything but unloved and unlovable? What other path was there for her?

It's okay Ava. I love you and you are going to be okay. I am here for you.

I am now watching fifteen-year-old Ava. She is exiting the school bus and very disturbed. She walks down the street to her family's apartment and opens to the door to find everyone home. In her hand is her report card for the quarter and on it is a C. It is the first C she has received in her life, and it is in geometry. Ava had begged her parents the entire quarter to let her stay after school to get extra help as her teacher was a lazy ass who taught the class from his chair only writing on the board as high as his arm would reach thus making learning the material extremely hard. She had asked her sister to help but she didn't have time for Ava. So, she received a C. Knowing this is not going to go well she decides to hand the report card to her mom to get the yelling over with.

"Ava, why did you get a C in geometry?"

"I don't understand it and my teacher doesn't explain it very well. I asked y'all for some help, remember?"

"No, you didn't."

Her dad snatches the report card away from her mother and stares at Ava.

Surely they remember her asking. She asked them if they would come pick her up after school so she could get help from one of the student tutors. They said no because she had committed to taking care of these two girls every day after school for a few hours and she needed to honor her commitment. Never mind that Ava had informed the parents of her need for a tutor and asked if it would be okay if her sister watched the girls for a few weeks and the parents said yes. Never mind she had explained this to her parents, and they said her sister was not going to do Ava's job for her. Ava is frustrated as she looks back and forth between her parents. She sees her sister out of the corner of her eye smirking at her.

"It's one fucking C," she yells as she stairs them down.

Her father moves closer to Ava not saying a word. When he is right in front of her he slaps her face. The blow is so hard Ava's head begins to ache. He slaps her again, and again, and again until her mom yells for him to stop.

"Where did you learn that word?"

Ava is now crying. She can't bring herself to look up at him.

"Answer me damn it!"

"From you," she cries out.

He reaches to slap her again and she ducks. This time her mom and her sister yell for him to stop.

"That is a fucking lie!"

"You just said the word!"

"Fuck you, Ava! Go to your room!"

Ava walks out of the kitchen and down the hall to her room. She stops first to use the bathroom and is shocked to see her face in the mirror. Both of her cheeks are dark red. Her head is still hurting and there is ringing in her ears. She wipes the tears from her face and mumbles, "but you do use the word you fucking asshole."

Oh my God Ava! You are so brave and smart! I am so sorry for this hurtful experience! I am here for you, and I love you so much!

Next, I see seventeen-year-old Ava. She is sitting on the floor of her bedroom listening to her boombox with her headphones on. She looks up to see her dad entering her home. She pulls the headphones just above her ears and watches as he takes a seat on the floor next to her. He says, "Your mother and I have been talking about this for a while and we have decided that when you get pregnant we are going to take the baby and raise it ourselves."

I see the look on Ava's face. She is confused by this statement as she is a virgin and has no intention of having sex and having a baby anytime soon. She is a senior in high school, is on the honor roll and barely leaves the house so this idea that she has been having sex is insulting to her. I see the tears forming in her eyes. She is both hurt and embarrassed. Why would they say this of their daughter? What had she done to make them think this was even a possibility? She however doesn't offer up the status of her virginity. Instead, she whispers, "okay" and pulls her headphones back over her ears. Her father gets up and leaves the room. As he closes the door the tears roll down her face. To be judged in such a way. Did they have this same conversation with her sister? She is certain the answer is no.

My sweet little Ava, it's okay. You are a wonderful, smart young lady and you deserve to be respected by your parents. It's okay though because I am here for you. Ava, you deserve so much more than what you are receiving from your parents but it's fine. I am with you now. I love you and will always be here for you.

Next I see young, college-aged Ava. This Ava is beat down and lonely. She has lived a life of hurt and disappoint. She has unsuccessfully muddled through twenty years thus far and is now traveling home on Spring Break with her dad. She listens to her dad tell her, "Ava, you are average. You will only get anywhere in life if you work hard."

She knows this is true, but the words don't sting any less. She tries to rationalize this train of thought with the fact that her parents grew up in the south, picking cotton, and they don't know anything but to work hard. And, while this makes her feel somewhat better, the words "you are average" continue to echo in her head. She's worked hard, earned an academic scholarship to Alabama State University, and turned down a scholarship to Auburn University (she was determined to go to an HBCU, but applied anyway to prove to her parents she would be accepted, and hell, she was offered a scholarship there too), has been successfully staying in the "honor zone" each semester, was an English tutor earning her own spending money until the school closed the program. Maybe that's a little above average since most people were not in college with such a scholarship. But it wasn't a full scholarship, so maybe he's right. She's getting As and Bs in accounting, and it's proving to be harder than her high school accounting class. Every semester, new professors encourage her to change her major to English, because she is so eloquent in every class where she has a writing assignment, but she's doing this damn accounting shit for these cotton-picking people. She's trying her best to prove herself worthy. She wants them to be proud of her, so she's stuck with this major, suppressing her desires, not bothering to even figure out what she can do with a degree in English– and for what? To be told she's average? Had she known this two years ago, she would have majored in English.

You are so much more than average dear sweet Ava! You are smart, funny, kind. Do not be hurt because they can't see you for who you are. I see you and I love you!

"Can you tell me about a memory when you were in your mid-twenties?"

"Yes, I came home to visit my family. While we sat in the living room, my mom informed me that everything good that had happened to me she and my dad thought would have happened for my sister. They didn't expect anything good to happen for me."

"How did that make you feel?"

"Shocked. I was shocked that she would admit it, but not shocked they felt this way. At this point, my heart is heavy with years of these types of statements from my parents."

I work through the process of giving this twenty-five-year-old Ava love, and I'm feeling better and stronger. I'm mama Ava, and I have work to do to keep these baby Avas safe.

"This has been exceptionally good. I'd like to ask you to think back to before you were born. Can you remember this?"

"Um, no, I don't think so."

"Just continue to relax and try, if you'd like."

"Okay."

My body begins to feel lighter and it's as though I'm floating by this point. I love this feeling, and I wish I could stay in this state forever. I remember my time in the womb. I begin to speak, "She doesn't love me, and she doesn't want me. I am growing inside of a woman who resents me."

"Do you know why you decided to be born to this woman, to this family?"

"Yes, I do. I needed these experiences to grow to the person I was meant to be, so I would have the compassion I need to help others, so I could better relate to others. I was brought to this world to help heal others."

"That's wonderful that you can remember this. Are you ready to wake up now?"

"Yes."

"Okay."

Amy guides me out of the hypnotic state I've come to love. As I return to the here and now, still lying on the table, I've reached yet another a strange level of peace – more peaceful than yesterday's session. I'm going to have to really take this all in, I guess. I don't even know how long I've been here, but I do know I feel stronger, more alert and there's this peaceful breeze sweeping over me.

I'm back on the train, feeling great and still bewildered. That was it. We had this hypnotherapy session, and now I feel great, and I don't really know why. I don't believe I am going to go out and make some major life changes, but I do feel a sense of confidence I didn't have before. Maybe it's the new mama bear in me, my new role of protecting my little Avas. Whatever it is, I love it, and it is a high I am thankful to experience this week.

Facebook, September 24, 2015
Yeah, she did that! She went 100% natural!!!

I've toyed around with the "big chop" as they call it for a couple of years now, and today I finally did it. I feel good, though not as liberated as I thought I would. I'm having a flashback to Angela Bassist's character in the movie *Waiting to Exhale*. She was going through a divorce and did the liberating haircut. She had that super short, sleek, relaxed look – it was hot! In my case, I did the chop, and what lied beneath months of weave was all natural me. I have very coiled hair. I am not sure I knew this. My hair stylist was marveling at my curl pattern, and shocked that I wasn't aware of what it was. I do recall being able to wash and blow dry my hair as a teenager, so I guess since I did it with ease, it would be considered on the side of, as we Black folks say, "good hair." I'm sure Chris Rock would cringe at those words! Maybe I should have chopped and relaxed it, but that would defeat the big chop experience. The big chop is all about going back to beginning – back to your natural state. I now have about a half inch of hair on my head, and I'll be rocking this look for a while.

So here I am, staring at myself after my selfie and Facebook post. I must admit this big chop does come with the removal of some baggage. I think it's the energy and hypnotherapy sessions that's got me in the "do me" mode, and I do love it!

It's been about two weeks since those sessions and I am incredibly happy. I'm loving it here in Santa Monica, and I love that I am one hundred percent living in the moment and engaging in my writing career. I've joined a writing club that is just around the corner from my apartment and connecting with these people has lit a spark in me! Hearing their stories of leaving their careers, many moving here from various parts of the country all to pursue their writing careers. Granted many want to be in the Hollywood world and write movie scripts but all the same we are writers. And surprisingly, many are my age and older. People who finally decided it was time to live life on their terms and did!

And Dan, well, I haven't given him much thought. He has crossed my mind, but the urge to reach out to him is not there anymore. Amy said the hypnotherapy would help with my self-esteem and she was right. I love that I'm accepting and not trying to rationalize any of this – the trip back to D.C., my time spent with Amy versus at the Annual Leadership Conference, cutting my hair, no lingering thoughts of Dan…it is like it's just supposed to be happening this way. Maybe it's because I'm stuck in right brain mode. I can't help but wonder though how things would be different if I were still able to switch back and forth. Would I be buried under tons of research at Big Brains, or would

I have had the thought to click to right brain and just live this way while out here in Southern California? I'll never know, but I do believe this was God's plan, and everything is happening the way it's supposed to. Monique is going to die when she sees my hair! I'll send her picture tonight.

11

Doing Me

Facebook, October 3, 2015
Wine tasting and the opera on the pier! What a wonderful Saturday!

I sent an email to the other Fellows at Big Brains to see if anyone wanted to join me, but I didn't get any takers. I'm kind of glad I didn't. I have a love for being alone. I'm not a hermit (as Al pointed out back at Shawshank), but I most certainly do enjoy doing things solo.

They say it's a good thing to be comfortable with yourself, but I sometimes think I really enjoy it way too much. In either case, a few samples of wine and a funny opera playing on a giant screen on the pier is a wonderful way to spend some alone time. Though, as I look around it would also make for a great date night. There are couples cuddled up with blankets wrapped around them and they seem so happy, so in love. I'm sitting on a beach chair with an ocean blue sarong wrapped around my legs. I am alone and I'm happy. I haven't thought about dating while I am out here, other than my dream of running into my masturbation man, Shemar Moore. Knowing I am only here for a year makes dating seem pointless, and I think this is a good time to just date myself. So here I sit on the pier surrounded by hundreds of people and feeling happy and secure with myself.

The Opera was nice though I only stayed for the first performance. I knew today was going to be an early rise and I wanted to make sure I was well rested. A few of the Fellows from Big Brains thought it would be great if we went for a hike in the Santa Monica Mountains. I was one hundred percent up for this experience as it is on my things to do this year list. I even found my way to the sporting goods store the other night to purchase a pair of hiking boots. That's one thing about me I love! I am all about the "outfit." If it's something that requires a "look" I'm going all in! Years ago, I went canoeing on the Illinois river and I showed up looking like I'd canoed many times before. Cut off shorts, a white t-shirt tied in a knot with a navy plaid long-sleeved shirt on top and, brand new navy Keds. I looked like I could be the token black chick in the sporting goods catalog. Funny thing about it was I couldn't swim to save my life and when the canoe flipped over my saving grace was the river was not that deep, so I didn't look too foolish as we worked to turn it back over and get in.

Today I am dressed in my "hiking" outfit which consist of khaki cargo pants, a sweat absorbency short-sleeve shirt with a gray hoodie wrapped around my waist for the cuteness effect because it is too hot to even think about wearing it, my light blue hiking boots, and a cute khaki baseball cap. I am going for the I do this all the time and don't feel the need to have my clothes coordinate look.

I am dressed and ready to go. I check my phone one last time before heading out the door. It's raining and I am thinking our hike may get canceled. No texts so let's do this thing!

As I pull into the parking area I see Tammy's car. I park next to her, grab my backpack and head over to say hello. To my surprise she is not in her car. I hear barking and turn to see her with her chocolate Labrador Retriever.

"Hey Ava!"

"Hey!"

"Who is this?"

"This is Maxi!"

"Hi Maxi!"

Maxi walks up to me, jumps up and licks my face.

"Oh, she is so sweet!"

"You have dogs, right? Why didn't you bring them?"

"My dogs are a poodle and yorkie and they would not be able to hang for a hike like this."

"Yeah, this would wear those babies out!"

I bend over to give Maxi a pat on the head and as I do two move cars pull up.

"That must be Stan and Will."

"Great, is it just the four of us?"

"Yes, the others backed out so just us."

"That's too bad."

I take a quick glance at Tammy's attire. She is wearing khaki cargo shorts and a t-shirt. She has done this many times before, so I feel I have successfully achieved the "hiking" look. Tammy is tall, maybe 5'10 inches and has a short pixie haircut. She is very pale, and her beach blonde hair enhances her lack of melanin.

As Stan and Will park I see there is a woman in the car with Stan so looks like there's five of us.

Stan and Will are Navy Fellows and are a blast to be around. They turn our weekly mandatory lunches which are already fun into a comedy show.

Stan and the woman get out. Stan is about six feet tall, with curly red hair and a face full of freckles. He too is in his mid-forties like me. The woman looks to be in her thirties and my height but is maybe 100 pounds. She seems so frail, slender tan face, skinny arms exposed from her short-sleeve hot pink t-shirt. I can't see her legs as she is wearing long black cargo pants.

"Hello everyone! This is my girlfriend Toya."

We give a group hello just as Will walks up with his dog a cheerful Border Collie.

"Hey! Are we ready to go? Sally is too!"

Will is in his thirties and an all-around athlete. He runs, bikes, hikes, swims. He is about 5'10', with dark brown hair and a body that looks like it belongs at the Olympics doing any sport he wanted to compete in.

"Yep, we're ready," Tammy gives an over-the-top response, and we begin making our way up the mountain with the rain spitting on us as we ascend.

It has been fifteen minutes and I am about to die! This trial is rated as moderate and my personal trainer, Greg, said this would be easy for me. I'll have to let him know he was kind of wrong. If I am breaking into a sweat after fifteen minutes I think I should be on the "for people who only dress like they do this but never have trail." Fortunately, I get to play it off much like my canoeing experience because Toya is moving slower than I am. We are pulling up the rear chatting and laughing and so it appears we are just casually making our way behind the others, but I can hear the exhaustion in her voice just as clearly as I can hear it in mine. We have bonded in these few short minutes.

About an hour in we stop for a break. The dogs are running around stopping for a short second to take a drink of water and the rest of us are sitting on large rocks eating power bars and drinking water. I may not be a pro at this but damn this sure feels great! The rain has stopped, and the sun is beaming brightly now. I look down at my brand-new shoes which are now covered in mud. I don't care as it symbolizes a new experience for me, and it makes my outfit look even more legit.

"Okay! Breaktime is over," Tammy yells, and we gap our things and continue our hike.

Until today I had forgotten I much I love being outside. Sure, the girls and I are at the park every day and I do run on the beach trail, but this is right smack in the thick of it all. As we continue to ascend the mountain we spot a pack of mountain lions in the distance. Toya and I who are chatting it up are only about 20 feet behind the others but seeing those mountain lions who are at best a half a mile away makes me wish we were closer to the group. Not to mention the dogs. Oh, dear God please keep the dogs safe. I notice I am the only one who seems to have any concern though. Will pointed them out. We all looked over, saw them and everyone is just continuing to hike on up this mountain. I guess I shouldn't be concerned either. Worse case they come after us and we die. I can think of less eventful ways to go.

Finally! We are at the top! Three hours later and we are here! The view is breathtaking. As we stand at the peak we begin to take pictures of the scenery and the town below. I have no idea what town or city it is. We are in the Santa Monica Mountains, but the landscape below appears to be a beautiful stretch of farmland. I am thankful for this day, for this experience, for Toya being as out of her element as I am. I learned a lot about her on this hike like she was born and raised here in Los Angeles. Her father is Asian, and her mother is Italian. Her name is of neither origin. Her mother worked with a lady name LaToya, and she liked the same but only the Toya part. She went away to college at a small private school in Boston but returned after one year as she is a West Coast girl and did not like the cold East Coast winter. She and Stan met about a month ago when he went to the Getty a place that is also on my must do while here list. The story of their meeting reminds me of the fairy tale I used to dream of when I first moved to the DMV. I would fantasize about meeting a handsome man at one of the museums, he'd ask me to join him for coffee at a nearby shop and we'd hit it off and live happily ever after. It didn't happen in the DMV though I did go to many museums always to see the new exhibit and always hoping to meet "the one." Maybe I too can have a Getty moment. Maybe there's nothing wrong with dating this year. Keep it light and simple knowing I may stay, may get shipped back to Shawshank or may end of someplace else. That seems to be Stan's approach and he and Toya seem great. I guess they are even though he chose to keep up with Will and Tammy today instead of walk with Toya but maybe he would have slowed his pace for her had I not be pulling up the rear with her. He seems like one of the good guys so I am guessing he would have chosen to walk at her pace had she not had my company today.

Our descent from the 3111-foot peak was much easier and I was happy for this swift journey back to our cars. I am beat but the day was exactly what I needed. Fresh air, and motivation about my dating life.

Facebook, October 4, 2015
Today I climbed the highest peak in the Santa Monica Mountains which is 3111 feet!

Facebook, October 10, 2015

Had fun mixing and mingling with people in the film industry tonight!
Have I mentioned I'm loving it out here 😎 - Promenade Playhouse

I don't want to return to the DMV – I've applied for so many jobs but only with wishful thinking but now I want this to be reality. I want to stay here. Tonight, was wonderful. I met so many people from around the world – from Australia to St. Louis. They all have a dream of making it here in L.A. They write, act, dance. They have passion that invigorates my soul. These people who were once insurance salespeople, or preschool teachers, are now here, and they've committed themselves to their dreams. I once had such dreams – not to be an actor, or a big part of Hollywood, but to write, and for my work to be made into a Hallmark movie. That dream is still in me and is renewed with each function I attend. It's like you can't help but catch the spirit of creativity. I've dusted off my writings since joining the writing club and I'm back in the flow. I've even had my work reviewed by an exclusive writing club president and was given great feedback. He said I had a voice, and that means to the world to me. While they don't have room in the club for another member, he encouraged me to stay in my current club and to check back with them next year. Next year! The idea that I would still be here next year, in my zone writing and thriving in my craft. It's possible!

As I head out of the playhouse and walk back to my apartment, I see my phone light up inside my purse. I pull the phone out and see it's a text from Dan.

Thanks for the birthday card. I appreciate you thinking of me.

I can't stop staring at the text, as if somehow it's going to say more than that. It won't and I shouldn't have sent the card in the first place.

Dan's fiftieth birthday was a couple of days ago, and I felt the need to send him a card. I didn't want to text, and I convinced myself it was because, while we had parted ways on bad terms, sending him a card was the right thing to do. Fifty is a big deal. Deep down I knew I sent the card because I wanted to let him know I cared, and it was fine if I never heard back from him. Sending a text seem to indicate I expected a reply, while mailing a card somehow doesn't warrant a response. This way, I wouldn't be setting up my little Avas for disappointment. There was also a part of me that was concerned that the hypnotherapy didn't work, or was wearing off, because if it were still working, I wouldn't even be thinking about him in the first place. But, after five years, it's hard to forget a person. A part of me also rationalized that this was a way to make peace with our separation, and to let him know there were no hard feelings.

I continue to glance down at my phone as I walk into my building. He's written no more, and I know if I just say, "you're welcome," this will end all communication with him. I know this is what needs to happen, and what's more interesting is I'm completely at peace with this understanding. I had a little tug in my heart last week as I set out to find a birthday card for him, but now, with another week passing, I am feeling somewhat indifferent. Hum, maybe the hypnotherapy is working? I don't know that I have much of a feeling about that, either. I mean, I care, but I'm not in a panic that I'm somehow losing the impact. I am just observing my thoughts, which is new to me. I normally overanalyze everything and digress into a rabbit hole. Thank goodness I can't switch over to left brain mode, or I'm sure I would. But, then again, in this new state would I bother to make the switch?

12

Shawshank...Again

Facebook, October 14, 2015
Quick trip to DC-in on Tuesday out on Wednesday! Will catch you all
on the next trip!

Back in Shawshank for a quick moment, but somehow it feels different. I've only been gone three months. I feel like a free slave wandering back in the building. I've got my freedom papers in my pocket, and I'm here to visit my still-enslaved family. I know I'll have to return in a few months if I don't land a job in California and this changes my thought of freedom papers to a permission note -like a slave with a note from her master saying she has permission to travel to town. My note comes in the form of TDY orders. But, just the same, I feel exceptionally relaxed swiping in for my meeting. I came back for a meeting with Big Brains – to meet with one of our Air Force customers – but since I'm here, I am going to interview a few folks from the Marines for my research paper on Security Cooperation.

After this meeting I'm heading over to Amy's for a session. This was an incredibly quick trip, for which I'm thankful, as I don't like being away from the girls for long periods of time.

As I exit the elevator, I expect to see Amy, but she is not at the front desk. I walk up to the receptionist to inform her of my appointment and as I do she appears from around the corner.

"Hello Ava!"

"Hi Amy! How are you?"

"I am well and yourself?"

"I am doing excellent!"

"That is wonderful to hear! Come, let's get started."

I follow Amy down the hall. This time she opens a door on the right side of the hall which is just across from the room we used the last time I was here.

"Please have a seat."

This room is similar to the other only it is a bit smaller. The head of the massage table is just about two feet from the door and the there are two wooden chairs about a foot away from the massage table. The room is painted a pale pink and there is a small writing desk in the opposite corner of the room.

"So, what's been going on?"

"A lot! I am really loving my life in Santa Monica, and I am hoping to stay after the fellowship."

"Wow, that is amazing. Your energy is radiating Ava! You are still very much in balance from your last Reiki session and the hypnotherapy."

This is good news for me. I wanted to check in with Amy as some kind of tune up or something. I am not sure how often I should, and she said I would just know. I will admit I am still feeling great, but I couldn't pass up the chance to see her while I was in town.

"Thank you! I appreciate knowing this; I do feel great."

"Ava, have you ever considered being a Lightworker?"

"I am not aware of what that is."

"It is someone who has been placed on this earth to be of service others. I have felt from the first time we met that you are a healer. And your revelation during your hypnosis session, that you are here to help and heal others tells me this is indeed true."

"Oh, okay well I am not sure how I would help other people. I think I still need to just help myself."

"I can understand your thinking. I will say us healers are usually the ones who are healing our own wounds. We tend to have all kinds of issues as they say. It's as you noted during your session the reason we are chosen or rather why our souls chose these lives is to learn and grow from our hurt and to then help others."

"That does sound like a beautiful offering for others. I am not sure though, but I will think about it.

"If you are ever ready I am happy to train you."

"Okay, thanks."

I smile at Amy, but I am terribly confused. Train me? Train me to do what? I am fresh out of therapy and not because it worked but because I chose to take a break from it. This Reiki and hypnosis stuff is cool but who am I to be of service to others?

"I am receiving some messages for you."

Amy stands and is now saying a prayer over me.

"Your Ascended Masters are giving you some advice. They say yes, it is good for you to stay in California, and it is possible if that is would you want to do."

"Okay," I whisper.

I must admit, this session feels quite different from either of last month's sessions. It's almost as if this is just what's going on in my life and having someone pray over me and communicate with Ascended Masters (whoever they are) are normal occurrences for me. I want to ask who or what are Ascended Masters, but I think I won't. Some spirits or something from the spirit world is telling me it's okay to stay in California! That's good enough for me. I'll do an internet search and find out more about them later.

"Ava, you are on a powerful spiritual journey and your Ascended Masters want you to know a lot will be changing for you."

"Really?"

"Yes. Might I offer you some reading suggestions?"

"Yes, of course."

"Autobiography of a Yogi" by Paramahansa Yogananda and "Mornings with the Masters" by Carol Richardson. I think you will find these to be of great support.

"Thank you, Amy. I will be sure to start reading these."

"You are most welcome."

"Amy, would it be possible for you to do energy readings or Reiki for my dogs? I recall you saying you help animals too."

"Why yes, of course!"

"Oh, yeah! How does that work?"

"I can do their session as a distance session. We don't have to be in the same room. Energy travels everywhere you know."

"Sure."

I had never thought about this, but she is correct. This should be interesting.

"If you would, please send me pictures of them. This will help me to connect with them."

"Okay, I will and thank you so much."

"I will check in with them later today and I can give you a call tomorrow to discuss their session with you."

"That is great, thank you. Should I pay for all of this here or is the animal session different?"

"We will count your session today for the dogs' session tomorrow since you didn't need any energy healing and didn't use all of your time today."

"Why thank you so much Amy!"

"You're welcome!"

We head out of the room and down the hall where Amy leaves me to settle my bill.

"Remember to have a quiet evening."

"Well, I will be meeting my friend Sheryl for dinner, but it should be nice and relaxing."

"Oh, well okay that should be alright just be sure to keep the conversation light."

She leans over and gives me a hug. Her embrace is warm and electrifying. I love her embrace and I feel the need to hold on longer, but I resist. I don't want to appear to be clingy or crazy.

So far my day has been very pleasant. I am happy to with my session or rather prayer time and Amy gave me good news about staying in California. I'll be sure get those books she mentioned and learn more about Ascended Masters. I could have just asked Amy but there was something telling me not to ask but that I needed to do my own research and then have a discussion with her about them.

I am now on the Metro heading to Chinatown for dinner with Sheryl. Maybe I should have canceled but Sheryl will be the first of my friends I've seen since I left a few months ago. This is my third trip back and she is only person I am meeting up with. I have enjoyed the break from my friends, but this is the third time I've returned, and I posted about it on Facebook so I think I should make an effort to see someone. Plus, we are meeting at my favorite steak restaurant in Chinatown.

As I head up the escalator I hear my name, "Ava!"

I look up and see Sheryl waving her arms wildly. I move from standing on the right to walking on the left of the escalator and I feel the huge smile that has made its way to my face.

"Hey girl!"

"Hey! I almost didn't recognize you! Where is your hair?"

"It's right here! That was someone else's hair, so I decided to detach it from my body."

"Ava you are crazy! Are you ready for dinner?"

"I am. I'm starving!"

We make our way down 7th St NW and arrive at the restaurant.

Once we are seated we both begin to speak. We stop and laugh, and I yield to Sheryl who then yields to me. I smile and motion for her to go first.

"Tell me all about it! Have you seen any celebrities, been to Beverly Hills?"

"A few celebrity sightings, I think though someone at Big Brains said it's hard to recognize them when they are in their regular people mode, jeans, t-shirt, no makeup. And, yes, I had to drive through Beverly Hills! Oh, my goodness! It's not what I imagined but it's nice."

"Nice? That's it?"

"Yeah, the houses are huge, but you can't really see them for the gates and tall trees. The cars parked in the front are regular cars. It took me a minute to realize these are the cars of the staff! Mainly I have just been chilling. I go to work don't do much there and then come home, take the dogs to the park and workout with my personal trainer a few times a week."

"You are looking good girl!"

"Thanks! I wanted to use part of my time this year to get back into shape. But, yeah not doing too much other than trips to the beach since it's so close -just taking it all in. I think the session I had with Amy helps me to be in this chill mode out there and I just met with her again today so I will be in a good state for some time to come."

"Who?"

"Amy, the lady we met earlier this year at the Integrative Healing Center, IHC."

"Oh, how is she?"

"She is great, and the session was amazing! It was much shorter than the previous one, but I received some great information from my Ascended Masters."

"What now?"

"Oh, I haven't spoken to you about my trip out here the other month."

"No, you've kind of ghosted all of us but we get it."

"You do?"

"Sure. Ava you're different. Not in a weird way but just not like us. We all knew you needed to escape from this area for a while, so it makes sense that you have gone off the radar. Don't worry we really do get it, and no one is offended."

Sheryl gives me a wink.

"Wow, I didn't realize everyone knew this. I am just figuring it out."

"I think you knew but you wanted to keep holding on. Holding on to your current position and working with those crazy people in OSD, holding on to Dan, holding on for everyone but losing yourself in the process."

Damn. Sheryl is one hundred percent right. She is one of the few who know the truth about Dan and even with her I tread lightly with how much I to tell her.

"So now Ascended what?"

"Ascended Masters. I am not really sure who they are, but I take it they are like spirit guides or something. I plan to read more about them. Anyway, they said I can stay in California if I want!"

"They did, huh?"

I see the smirk forming on Sheryl's face. And I bust out laughing.

"Yes! Okay I know I don't know what I am talking about, but I am telling you this energy thing is real! The other month my session with Amy was incredible -the feelings, the vibrations, the sense of peace. I am telling you I am in a much better place than ever! And I've been reading this book on Angels. I've been seeing all kinds of feathers and I am not sure why, but I felt like I was supposed to look this up – what it means when you see different color feathers. I did and it led me to this book. Plus, with the energy sessions or Reiki I think I should just call them that, I am feeling like I am opening up to some really amazing ways to work through the problems in my life. It's feeling more helpful than therapy has ever felt."

"Ava, girl, that's all good, but just remember to keep God first. Angels can be sent by the Devil you know."

I should have known.

"Well, I always pray that only the ones sent by God enter my life. I'm good."

"I'm not saying I don't believe in this. I'm just saying be careful."

"Yep. So, what's new with you?"

Sheryl proceeds to tell me about a new guy she's met and how this one might be "the one." I'm half-listening, as I'm trying not to engage too much and stay relaxed. Listening to Sheryl go on about some dude can be anything but relaxing. She goes on for what feels like hours about all the materialistic aspects of the guy, and then finds a way to conclude he's probably not the one. It's been this way since I've known her. I want so much to tell her she has commitment issues, but what's that part in the Bible about taking the speck out of your eye first?

There have been many calls I've made while sitting in the courtyard of the Pentagon – from doctor appointments, to using my lunch break to make calls about my dog walking business, but never could you have convinced me I'd be on the phone getting the results of an energy reading for my dogs. Amy texted me last night to let me know she had connected with Cleo and Sophie, and we have selected 1 PM as the time she is to call with information from their session.

I've just wrapped up my meeting with the Marine guys and have made it to the courtyard. My thoughts of this being like a prison yard are still the same only I know after this call I get to be free of this place as I am heading to the airport to fly back home this evening.

My phone rings and it's Amy.

"Hello Amy! Thank you for calling."

"Hello Ava, you are welcome. I want to tell you Cleo and Sophie are delightful! I had a wonderful session with them, and they are doing really well for their ages."

I take a deep breath. I know my girls are getting older, but I want to believe they will live to be at least twenty years old. I honestly don't know how to conceive of a life without them in it.

"Cleo has some minor health issues. For starters she has too much acid in her body but that can be easily fixed. I will send you some information on how to reverse this. Also, she has some joint issues. If you can purchase a ramp for her to use for the couch and the bed she would be so thankful!"

"Okay, yes I will thank you. She feels okay though?"

"Oh, yes! She is feeling great, and she is loving the West Coast! Sophie is a little sad. She doesn't understand why you have to leave them sometimes."

My heart aches from hearing these words. I think I've left them more this year than any other time in their lives. And, I am not going someplace wonderful and exciting, I am simply returning to the DMV.

"My poor baby!"

"It's okay Ava. I explained to her that you have to take business trips and that they have been helpful for you personally as well and she understood."

"Thank you for that, I appreciate it."

"You're welcome. There is a way to send them love while you are away from them. Let's walk through that process now."

Amy gives me instructions on how to telepathically send love to the girls from afar and as we do so I can feel my heart warming. I can feel them with me as though they are right here in the courtyard with me. Hold on babies! Mommy will be home tonight!

13

Back Home

Facebook, October 24, 2015
Just finished an awesome spin class and took a swim lesson this morning! About to meet up with some folks and eat whatever I want 😊

I have been a *The Young and the Restless* fan since I was a kid, so to see Eric Braden (aka Victor Newman) stroll up to the restaurant where Tammy and I were having dinner blew me away! It was a nice ending to what turned out to be a torturous day. Who knew swimming would take so much out of me? While I thought I was rested, I clearly was not, because twenty minutes into my spin class and I thought I was going to fall off the bike. Plus, I haven't attempted to swim since my ninth-grade gym class. When I was four years old, my mom signed us up for swim classes and they were not successful in teaching me how to swim. Every class, I clung to the instructor, and if not her, the side of the pool. Needless to say, I didn't learn how to swim, and viewed that summer a one of my worst. I recall thinking my mom must not have liked me, because she could clearly see I hated going to swim classes, yet she never failed to take my sister and me every week. Funny, this memory didn't come to me during my hypnotherapy session with Amy, but I can see it's part of the many events that have shaped me and my view of my family. What's that Dr. Phil says? It's about your perception of things. It doesn't matter what others' intensions were, it's how I've perceived things throughout the years. I would have to guess my mom made us take swim lessons because she thought it was a good thing, not because she hated me. She's not the most talkative or affectionate person, so I can see why there was never a moment of, "Oh honey, I'm doing this so you can be safe near the water, and someday you'll want to hang out with your friends and go to the pool. You'll be able to participate and have fun."

No, that was never going to be something I'd hear from her, so, as a four-year-old, I interpreted it as torture.

Now here I am every Saturday morning with a sixty-three-year-old classmate shivering in this cold ass water, but the days are gorgeous. The fact that I'm taking swim lessons in November in an outdoor pool is incredible. The fact that my classmate is sixty-three shows me I'm still young, yet at learning something new. I've never counted ninth grade gym class as learning, though I did manage by the end of that semester to jump into the deep end and swim on my back to the other side of the pool. I never swam after that, so I've assumed that miraculous feat of jumping into the deep end and making my way to the other side was a fluke.

Nonetheless, I show up every Saturday morning ready to learn. I would have thought I'd be nervous, but I'm not. My classmate is always ready to go, goggles and swim cap on, blowing bubbles into the water. I, of course, am outfitted in my expensive swimsuit and vest wetsuit. One more thing to cross off my bucket list.

So, to recap today, swim class, first spin class in my life, and sitting five feet away from Victor Newman – all in one day! I'm good for a while!

Facebook, November 3, 2015
Waiting to be a part of The Real
studio audience!

Facebook, November 3, 2015
Had a fun time at The Real!

Facebook, November 3, 2015
Another picture! Had a wonderful
time and I won a t-shirt for my
Instagram page!

Every time I think I've reached the peak of excitement out here in the L.A. area, I go a little further. I am a huge fan of the talk show *The Real*. One of the first things I did when I found out I was coming here was find out how to get tickets for the show. Today's guest was Kelly Osbourne, and that was nice, since I know who she is. I was hoping there would be a guest I'd know, and I lucked out. The mystery of how a television show is taped was unveiled, but I'm sure that's to be expected. I didn't realize there were so many moving parts, and that there's a hype guy to keep the audience excited. I couldn't help but imagine someday being a guest and sitting next to the ladies on the couch and discussing one of my books. Loni Love is, after all, one of my inspirations. She went from an engineer, to a comedian, to a talk show host. I look to her and think, "Yes, you can have your heart's desire." When prompted by the show to use Instagram to participate in the activities of the day, I quickly created one, and gave myself the username avayesican.

My only regret today was not speaking up when one of the producers asked if any of us had a question for Loni. We were waiting in line to enter the studio, and this guy says, "Hey! Anyone have any questions for Loni today?" Oh, yes, I did! But I froze. I did this once before with Toni Morrison at the National Book Festival. I could have been the first up to the microphone to ask my question. After all, I made a point of getting there extra early and sitting right next to one of the microphones so I could easily pop up and ask my question. When the time came for audience questions, my heat started pounding, and I couldn't move. Marva was with me that day. She nudged me to move, but I glanced at her and gave a quivering smile. Afterwards, as we headed to the line to have our books autographed by Ms. Morrison, Marva asked, "Ava, what happened back there?"

"Oh, I just lost my nerve."

"But we got here at the crack of dawn to get those good seats."

"Yes, but I just couldn't do it. I got so nervous. I am kicking myself for it now."

"No need for that, the moment is over, and we did get to see her up close. There's goodness here."

"I guess you're right."

"I have to ask, what was your question?"

"My, question was: how does she manage to have a massive amount of uniqueness in each of her characters? You know, some authors' writings feel as though you are with the same set of characters, even though it's a different book, different characters, different city, different country but somehow the characters feel the same. The only thing that's different is the names. Ms. Morrison goes deep. From Sula to Violent, from Joe to Son. All remarkably different."

"Wonderful question! So thoughtful! She would have loved it I'm sure."

"Thanks, but now I just feel worse."

"Ah, honey, no need in feeling anything but happy to have seen one of your inspirations up close and personal. Now let's get these books signed!"

We waited in line for over an hour, and, to our dismay, Ms. Morrison had to leave before we made to the front of the line. Just another example of how I missed a moment. I swore after that I wouldn't let another opportunity slip by me again, but alas I did it today. Damn it!

Today, I came to the taping of *The Real* with, Tammy. She is a joy to be around. When I think of a Marine, I don't think of an essential oil using, hypnotherapist in training individual, but she is, and she's also raw. Tammy shoots straight from the hip. I kind of wish I were as ballsy as she is. There is another Fellow from the Navy who impresses me as well, Sarah. She is into yoga, Chakras, energy healing and crystals. Not to mention, one of the ladies who works at Big Brains has a cubicle full of gorgeous crystals – the large raw amethyst and rose quartz sparkle and catch my eye each time I pass her cubicle. She is the most pleasant human I've encountered in my life. I know this is no accident, and God aligned us all to meet at this time in our lives. I am now surrounded by people who have a wealth of knowledge about everything I was starting to take an interest in back in the DMV and they are happy to share with me.

My purpose for being here is clearly beyond that of this fellowship, beyond my career aspirations. In fact, I am beginning to think this fellowship was merely the vehicle to introduce me to all the things I need to finally find my way in this world. I have been lost since birth, and now, at forty-two, I am awakening and connecting with my soul. I am thinking about these coincidences. I most certainly will not take them for granted, and I won't let any more opportunities pass me by. I am surrounded by everything that was starting to mean something to me before I left the DMV. I may have missed my moment with Loni, but I won't miss any more moments in life. And I am damn certain I will be back on the set of *The Real,* and this time Loni will be asking *me* the questions!

Facebook, November 7, 2015
Enjoying a great day. Just ran into
the Honorable Jeh Johnson, Sec
Homeland Security!

Facebook, November 7, 2015
Air Force One! Got to tour this
one which was in service from
1973-2001.

I spent the day at the Ronald Reagan Presidential Library for a conference. While the conference itself was good, the tour of the museum was by far the best part of the day. I ended my day by paying my respects to President and Mrs. Reagan and looking out over the picturesque Simi Valley. The view was breathtaking. I remember watching Reagan's funeral on television years ago and seeing this very spot. Never in a million years did I think I'd be standing here. Having ended the tour, reading his Sunset letter, I was filled with love and a new perspective. To know you are entering a point in your life where you will slowly begin to forget family, friends, the love of your life – to know this and to write such an eloquent letter about it, I think most people would be so heartbroken they wouldn't want to talk about it, and most certainly wouldn't want to announce it to the world. What a brave man. After reading it, I began to reflect on my life. I haven't entered into any season of losing my memory, but I was exiting a season of losing my mind, and entering into a season of learning myself, getting to know my soul, my essence. Reagan must have been at this place to write that Sunset letter, a place of being connected with his core, his truth. I am glad I'm awakening to this new discovery. This new part of my journey has to offer more than I have experienced so far in my life.

Facebook, November 8, 2015
At the Pearl xChange conference. We are sitting at the table next to Nicole Richie the host and Cameron Diaz! Gwyneth Paltrow is the guest speaker!

Facebook, November 8, 2015
So, the evening ended with me running into Vanessa Simmons who shared some great business advice while waiting to meet Jeanette Epps.

Today was a good day! I am fired up from this conference! Marianne Williamson held nothing back and gave me that kick in the butt I needed to move forward as a female entrepreneur. I've put my business on hold since coming out here, but I'm inspired to dust it off and do some work. After all, it's a dog walking and pet sitting service that I plan to expand to a full-scale doggy daycare. What better place to learn about luxury for dogs and pampering them than here? I shared my elaborate concept with Vanessa Simmons, and she was so taken with it that she thought the business was already up and running! I told her I was only out here for a year, and she said I needed to stay and do my business here, as it was exactly what L.A. needed. Sure, they had doggy daycares, but they had nothing close to my daycare/coffee shop concept. I was moved, and I was close to asking if she thought her uncle Russell Simmons would like to be an Angel Investor, but I stopped short of doing so.

And, I just have to say, standing two people behind Cameron Diaz in the lunch line was incredible! The security guard asked her if she wanted to move to the front. She smiled, gave a little laugh, and said she was good waiting like everyone else. It's not the biggest deal but it was nice to see she's down to earth.

I came to this event with Sarah, the Navy Fellow. I found out about it via Twitter. There I was randomly scrolling through and there's this post from Nicole Richie. I feel like I belong here, like it was no accident that we were sitting one table over from some of Hollywood's elite. I look at it as a sign of what's next for me – even the glam part of it. I wore a navy blue tight-fitted knee-length dress (thank you, sales lady, for the tight tip), flesh-colored heels, and sported one of my Prada purses. And not that my baby Range is all that, but we did step out of a luxury car. I am so feeling this life!

Facebook, November 15, 2015
I went in for the basics, food, treats, poop bags...
and came out with these 😊 *The weather is*
getting a little chilly here and... they always
need new Christmas sweaters!

Okay, so I call Uncle! It does get chilly here! Not earmuff and Uggs chilly, though everyone around me is dressed like they're at Big Bear Mountain and not strolling down the Promenade. Yes, the breeze from the ocean adds a bit of a nip in the morning air, but by mid-day it's warm again, at least to me, but I've been surviving sub-zero temperatures in the DMV and, prior to that, ice storms in Oklahoma. I'd have to live here for years to acclimate and bundle up like these people.

Leisurely making my way down the Promenade and into the mall, I spot a homeless man and his dog who is adorned in a rhinestone collar, a doggy ski jacket and is people watching from her seat in a kid's wagon. I barley take a step pass them when the man calls out, "Hey, can you help me with a problem?"

I stop, turn, and see him holding an old, crumbled receipt.

"Sure, what's up?"

"I have this will from my mom, and you see here? She's left everything to me."

"Wow! That's great," I say peering at the receipt as if to read it.

"Yeah, but the problem is, I have to call my aunt and deal with her to get the money and she's a bitch."

"Man, I'm sorry about that, but if you can deal with her for just a while, you can collect your inheritance."

"Good point, but nope. I'd rather keep living on the street. She's such a bitch."

"I understand, and it's your call. You can wait and call her when you feel like dealing with her."

"Smart! That's what I'll do! Thank you! You have been such a great help!"

"You're welcome. And who is this?"

"This is Diamond."

"Hi, Diamond, you're a pretty girl!"

I give the dog a wave. Normally, I would pet it, but I guess I'm being a bit of bitch or a germaphobe, seeing how Diamond looks like she hasn't had a bath in an awfully long time.

"Say thank you, Diamond."

I watch him pet the dog's head then give her a kiss on the check. It's quite endearing and nothing different than I would do with Cleo and Sophie. I feel a smile coming across my face.

"Well, have a wonderful day!"

"You too ma'am!"

I wish I had some cash, but I don't. I wish I had some food for Diamond. I try to stop thinking about the pair as I ride the escalator to the food court in the mall, but I can't. It's such a shame and the homeless population seems out of control out here – much more than in the DMV. I'll be sure to start carrying some cash on me.

14

Introduction

Having a coffee shop right next to the company I'm working at is good, but bad for my hips. It's here that I usually see Chudney Ross at least once a week, intently staring at her laptop. I always want to walk up and say hello and let her know that I'm extremely impressed with her children's bookstore down the street, and that I'm an inspiring children's author myself, but every time I see her, I get nervous. Sometimes, she glances up from her laptop, and once or twice we've made eye contact. I never smile. I try to pretend as if I have no clue who she is. My rationale for not introducing myself is that I wouldn't want her to think that I'm just trying to meet her because she's the daughter of Diana Ross, who, by the way, is my most favorite entertainer in the world. As a child, I fantasized she and Billy Dee Williams were my real birth parents and that, any day now, they would come back and claim me. As I got older, I realized the timeline didn't add up, and that her daughter Tracee would kill that whole theory as she is just a few months older than me. But it was nice to fantasize, especially after just getting my ass whooped by one of my parents for doing something that, in my mind, was simply just being a kid. To them, mixing perfumes with lotion in the bathroom and trying to sell them to my sister, dad and mom was unacceptable and needed to stop, so I'd get a little beat down. By the next week I was mixing up my concoctions again. If they had of encouraged me instead of whooping me, I wonder if I would have become chemist, or something in the STEM world. Instead, they continuously beat me down. Anyway, I digress. The point is I should be able to say hello. What's the worst thing that could happen? She tells me she can't be bothered to speak. That's better than, "I can't trust you," or "the sex is bad," or any of the other hurtful things I've endured from Dan over the years. I'm sure I'll say hello before too long, after all, I pledged not too long ago to never let opportunities slip by me again – so it has to happen.

15

California State of Mind

There are many things I could be doing tonight – playing with the girls, writing, reading or just being a couch potato, but none of these things won out. Today, I took time from my not-so-busy evening and wandered up Santa Monica Boulevard to a quaint little bookstore. I've passed this store several times but never went inside. From a quick glance, I could see it was a spiritual bookstore, and by "spiritual" I mean the most noticeable thing inside was an exceptionally large statue of Buddha. No, not spiritual like my folks back in Alabama would think; in no way is it a "Christian" bookstore.

I've been searching for my space, my place where I can truly connect with God. Just two months ago, while back in D.C. for a conference, I found myself lying on a massage table in Friendship Heights receiving an energy reading and healing, which I now understand as Reiki, and undergoing Affect Bridge Hypnotherapy. And while I don't have the words for it, I know my soul is aching for newness. It requires more than Sunday morning church services, and more than counseling with a pastor would ever yield, and while the Reiki and hypnotherapy has worked, I know I have to find something to help maintain my new energy flow.

So, here I am on a random night in November by happenstance of seeing a local meet-up invite in my email. As I enter the Bolt of Lightning Spiritual Bookstore it is early, so I have a chance to look around. The store is dimly lit, small, and every space inside is covered with books, crystals, and essential oils; every element in this space has its own residence, or rather temporary residence, as it awaits its owner to claim it and give it a new home. The book titles alone seem to be filling my soul with a much-needed dose of love. From Chakra balancing to yoga practices to the healing power of crystals, they are all here, and they welcome me into this space.

I find the tiny staircase hidden at the back of the store. As I slowly climb each step, I look around and take it all in; downstairs now looks like a sea of books and artifacts with the beautiful statue of Buddha adding droplets of light to the room, and upstairs is still a mystery. As I make my way upstairs to the meeting area, I feel a sense of peace. No thoughts are entering my mind, no vibes that would normally help me realize I was out of my element. Nothing is urging me to head back downstairs and go home.

I find my place on the floor and wait for others to arrive. As I sit, waiting in this tiny loft area, I read more book titles, from Jesus to Karma. All of what anyone could ever think to find an interesting spiritual subject is here in this space.

She appears. Grace in form of a beautiful woman. She walks with ease; she smiles with ease. She seems to be floating around us though she has seated herself in front of the group on the floor. I can feel my soul devouring her essence. I want her peace and tranquility. I am hungry for her words, yet I feel a sense of patience as we wait for a few others to find their way to the floor. She then speaks.

"Good evening, my name is Nala." I'd like to share with you my story of transformation."

She tells of her discovery of meditation and the joy that now encompasses her life. She offers truth in the time and effort required to establish a good practice. She is done. She is brief with her words and yet it is so clear why I am here. I tried meditation in the past — bought a book, downloaded an App — but it didn't work.

After her talk I approach her. I need this now.

"Hello Nala, thank you for sharing your story today."

"It was my pleasure. I hope you found it helpful."

"I did indeed, and I would like to take your meditation class."

"That is wonderful. I have a form; would you mind filling it out?"

"Sure, of course."

She reaches in her bag and pulls out a sheet of paper.

"Looks like I forgot my clipboard."

She reaches back in her bag and pulls out a notebook.

"This should help."

She hands me the paper and the notebook, and I begin reading the form.

The questions are standard except for the last one which notes the classes are offered to all and payment is based on a sliding scale. Based on your income level, you select the price of the class. How thoughtful. I look at the income levels and see I am at the far right of the scale which is fine because I'll pay anything to get where she is. I wonder if Amy meditates. She too has a Zen-like presence. Amy's Zen is different though more like peaceful but in motion. Nala is more of a peaceful and stillness. But Amy must meditate to be as calm as she is or maybe she gives herself energy sessions. I wonder if you can do that? Give yourself energy healing. I'll have to look into that.

I complete the form and hand it back to Nala. By now the others have left and it is just us.

"Thank you, Ava. What a beautiful name."

"Thanks."

"When would you like to start?"

"As soon as you are able."

"I have availability next week. We can start next Tuesday."

"That works for me, thank you!"

"Of course. I will email you with some additional information before then."

"I am looking forward to this, thank you again."

"You are welcome."

Nala looks as if she has more to say but stops. I smile and begin to head downstairs. I've only been here four months and so far I've had several unique experiences from sessions with Amy to hiking a mountain to finally learning how to swim to this. God, I can't thank you enough for this!

Walking home, I am relieved. This is the missing link. I know it is. Nala was short and to the point about the benefits of meditation, but she didn't need to be long. I know this is what I need next in my journey. Everything is coming so easily to me since my Reiki session. I don't stress; I just *am*, and it just comes.

16

Vedic Meditation

It's seven o'clock and I'm a good fifteen minutes away from her home. I don't want to panic, as this is my first session and that doesn't seem like the best way to start a four-day mediation course. She said not to worry and to take my time, but I hate being late. I left my place over an hour ago thinking I had more than enough time. I hate L.A. traffic, yet this city has grown on me, and I know I should stay here after my fellowship ends.

The GPS has directed me to take a right. I am now on her street, just need to find a place to park. Okay. I'm only ten minutes later than our start time. Somehow this makes me feel better, but I am certain it stems from deep rooted insecurity.

I park and hop out, looking at my handy work. I am usually all kinds of wrong when it comes to street parking. I never did master parallel parking. As I approach the door, I see a sign asking guests to remove their shoes. As I begin to remove mine, she appears. I am now seeing her, as the other night I only felt her. She is tall, maybe five feet ten inches or so. Her long blonde hair is flowing around her face as if there is a breeze, and her eyes are as blue as the Caribbean Sea. I believe she is wearing sari, or at least I think that's what they are called. The dress is burnt orange. This color coupled with her blonde hair and blues eyes makes me think of sunset on the beach. She's doing it again, that ease of her smile, that floating sensation that I've never felt around another human being before. Oh, please, God, let me get this good vibe; let it be a part of my existence after finishing this course.

I have brought a few items for our first session, as requested in her email to me — flowers, a white napkin, and a piece of fruit. I hand them to her, and she begins to explain the offering. After the offering, she begins to explain Vedic Mediation and its origins with Maharishi Mahesh Yogi.

I know I am awkwardly staring at her as she explains the history of Vedic Meditation. I feel this pull towards her, this sense of connection as she speaks. It's like the night at the bookstore, but tonight there's a feeling of assurance. I know this is my answer and my life will change even more after tonight.

As she whispers my mantra into my ear, my body vibrates. The sound is foreign and as I whisper it back, I stumble. She smiles and repeats it again. I attempt again, and she smiles again.

We end the first session with a meditation session. I close my eyes and allow my mantra to come to me. After some time, she tells me to let go of the mantra, and to continue to rest with my eyes closed. After a few minutes she informs me I can slowly open my eyes.

"How do you feel?"

"Good, peaceful. I did feel the numbness you noted."

"Good. Did you see anything?"

"No, just an almost paralyzing sense of stillness."

"That's good, especially for your first time. You can meditate on your own in the morning and we'll do your evening mediation tomorrow during your next class."

"Okay, great."

"You have such a peaceful energy."

"Really, I do?"

"Do you not think so?"

"I guess I thought I was always feeling rushed, but since moving here in July, yes, I guess I have less stress in my life. It makes me want to stay here and not return to the D.C. area."

"If that's what you want to do, you should do it."

"Yes, I should."

I smile as she walks me to the door. We hug and I walk outside. As she closes the door, I slip on my shoes, and I can feel the big grin making its way across my face. I don't know if it's the mediation or her exceptionally calm nature that has me so at ease. I just meditated and it felt amazing!

Something was happening to me, to my mind, my body, and my soul. I had felt the numbness on my lips as she said I might. I felt an overwhelming sense of peace and stillness.

It didn't take four sessions for me to start feeling the positive effects of mediation. At the end of each lesson, I was driving home singing along with the radio and radiating all kinds of positive energy. Nala was impressed with how quickly I took to the practice. She said most of her students normally didn't see such immediate effects. I am now seeing beautiful colors when I meditate, and I've transcended a few times. The transcending is amazing, indescribable. Nala explained transcendence as this space where there are no thoughts, where my higher self has connected with God/Source/Universe. She said the moment may be brief and once I've noticed I am in this space I am no longer in this space which makes sense. I love catching these moments! I've never done any type of drug, but I am guessing this is what it feels like to be high.

Twice a day for twenty minutes has drastically changed me. I want to encourage everyone to learn mediation. I can't imagine anyone's soul not needing this.

Facebook, November 26, 2015
Russell Simmons – the only time refugees killed real Americans in the country was the pilgrims…happy thanksgiving.

This has been my thought for years and the cool thing is I think like a mogul/philanthropist. For those who know that I am a true believer in signs I take this as a sign that I am still on the path to achieve greatness and give wonderful gifts to the world! Not that I had any doubts 😄 *. Oh yes, my throat chakra is open and firing off some stuff lately!!! Loving this uninhibited me!*

"Boo-Yah!" as the late Stuart Scott would have said. Well, maybe not about this subject, but I always loved his Boo-Yahs. I also had a mad crush on the man, but I will spare a digression moment. The point is, I'm so sick of all this refugee crap. Maybe we can't help everyone but how in the hell can we help no one? Let's not say is a money thing. I've been intimately involved in the Air Force's budget for my entire career, and I know we have more than enough – and that's just one branch within DoD and not counting the other federal agencies. I'm no senator or congresswoman, but I am open-hearted, and I know we have the money to help our brethren. Anyway, it just pisses me off.

Facebook, November 26, 2015
Well, looks like these two have left me hanging for the day 😊 *They had a big Thanksgiving breakfast and are out for the day -or until they*

decide it's treat time! I'm so thankful for these lil ones! Every day they bring me love and laughter 😊

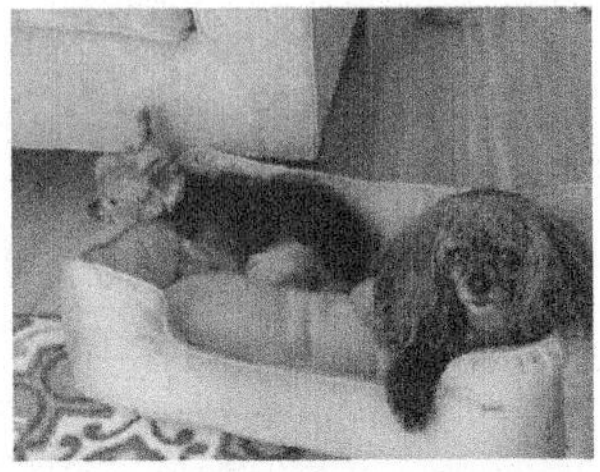

Facebook, November 26, 2015
Look who woke up! We were out for 2 hours and hit two parks and the pier! Now they're napping again so guess who's about to hit the beach...!!!

I'm surprised by the number of people at the beach today. The weather is nice enough, but it is a holiday so I guess there's only so much family and friends one can take on Thanksgiving. Most years, I am alone with the girls. Some years, I meet up with friends at one of the hot new restaurants in D.C., but I prefer the quiet of the girls and me.

I did reach out to my family, tried to convince them to come out for Thanksgiving or Christmas, but they all refused. I wouldn't turn down spending the holidays in California, but then again that's what makes us so incredibly different. They are hellbent on doing the same damn thing year after year. Alabama or bust! Missing Christmas with them last year was an unmoving experience for me. It's not that I don't love them, but I just don't connect with them in any way. I am sure they realize this, too, and that's why none of them are moved by my absence throughout the years.

I really am a loner, and it works fine for me. I would of course like a man, a life partner, a soulmate, but even then, I wouldn't want to do much with him. I'd want to stay in and keep him all to myself. My man and my baby girls. That's all I need.

Facebook, November 27, 2015
On our way out this morning for our walk there was a homeless lady and her dog sitting at the front of our building. She spoke, I spoke, and we went on our nice long walk. As we were returning, I was so excited to think about Cleo and Sophie modeling their new Christmas sweaters and when we got back to the front door she and her dog were still there.

Whenever I pass a homeless person on the street with a dog, I always say a prayer for the dog as my heart breaks for them so much. Not that I don't care about the person but it's because I see the homeless person eating food and I think that poor dog may get the scraps and is certainly not getting anything that's nutritious for them. So, when we got back inside, I went through the cabinets and pulled out dog food and snacks to take back down to the little guy. There's nothing in my cabinet that isn't good for him because Cleo and Sophie only eat the best food for sensitive stomachs with limited ingredients which are all organic and the list goes on . Then I grabbed all the cash that was sitting on the coffee table which wasn't much because I'm not a cash caring kind of gal, but I took that and dropped it in the bag as well and went back downstairs. I gave the dog one of the treats and spoke to the lady for a while and she looked in the bag she was very thankful.

I'm sharing this with you all as a reminder that we are all so blessed my Facebook family and friends and I know some of you go out of your way every day to help those in need and we are truly blessed to have you making that daily sacrifice. But for me my gift was small and there's not one thing that I gave today that I can't go out right now and replace 100 times over and it just makes me think as much as I want to do and my plan to do in

the future for homeless dogs and people there are little things I can do right now to start making a difference.

So, I'm asking whatever grabs your heart, whatever makes it break just a little do something this season and beyond to make that problem a little lighter in the world.

Have a wonderful holiday season!

Facebook, November 27, 2015
Earthing/Grounding - my newfound love! God's healing power! Wednesday, I woke up with a terrible pain in my neck. After getting a massage and taking pain meds I was still in bad shape. Then I thought of Earthing which I am just learning about and do on occasion. So yesterday I hit the beach and sat there for about 25 minutes and today all the pain is gone!

I picked up this incredible book and DVD at a bookstore in Topanga. Tammy and I ate there prior to seeing Thomas John, a Medium, on Halloween night. I couldn't believe I so easily said yes when she asked me to go with her. I've seen Mediums on television and have found their ability to communicate with the dead fascinating but have always been a bit on the skeptical side. I will admit having a live experience was incredible. He said he didn't know any of the people who were receiving messages and I believed him and them. Maybe it was the setting, Halloween night, in the mountains sitting in a beautiful bohemian decorated amphitheater that gave the experience more credibility or perhaps it was some of the questions people asked that altered my view on mediumship. There were a few people asking about their loved ones coming to them in their dreams and it made me think about my grandmother who has been doing this for some years now. I used to think they were just dreams but now I think she is perhaps reaching out to me from the beyond. Marva and I have discussed my connection with my grandmother before and she is a believer that one's soul can come to visit you. I've asked her about my grandmother showing herself as the wind blows as that being a sign of her presence and she said it was indeed. I'll have to see what she thinks about dreams.

Anyway, I digress. I am now an Earther if that is a word. After viewing the video and reading the book, I was a believer. Sheryl had mentioned Earthing once or twice before, but I really didn't pay her much attention. It's seemed like a wonderful concept, but I had so much on my mind especially as moving out here started to become a reality, that not much of what anyone said was registering with me. But Earthing now has a place in my heart and I love it! Now on my walks with the girls, I make of point of not just sitting in the park under a tree but ensuring some part of my body is touching the tree or the grass. I've even gotten brave enough to take off my shoes and let my bare feet soak in Mother Earth. It's not really a hard thing to do out here where there are people sleeping on the grass in the park (and not just the homeless people). There are people with book bags and brief cases who've stopped on the way home just for this. They take time for themselves and to allow for some restorative healing. I love living here!

Facebook, December 5, 2015
As I ease back into my business, I thought the best way to get in the spirit was with a holiday campaign and since I felt so good for helping the one homeless dog and their owner last week I decided to continue that spirit

of giving! I've helped a few more dogs and their owners over the last week and I am now asking others to help as well! Please spread the word!

Thanks!

I had decided not to work on the dog business while out here this year, but I've now decided I can tie the homeless dog campaign to my business, so that's what I'm doing. I have no intentions of walking dogs or doing any pet sitting. I just need to use the business name to run this campaign. I've made a pretty decent video and posted it on my business' YouTube page. It's called "the Homeless Dog Holiday Campaign." I'm not asking for money or any kind of donations, just that people take a few minutes and package up some of their dog's food and treats, and a few dollars for the pet owner and pass the package on to a homeless person with a dog. It's not much, but it's more than what they have. I got the idea for the video when I was speaking with a homeless lady the other day. I asked if I could record her and her dog and share their story. She told me how she had given most of her Thanksgiving meal to Werewolf, her dog, and it made him sick. I did some research and found that many homeless people will provide for their dogs before taking care of themselves. For this lady, I informed her perhaps too much human food was not good for Werewolf, her twenty-pound little buddy, and perhaps he needed dog food. I asked if she'd be there for a while and she said yes, so I hurried down the street to the ATM, took out twenty bucks, and then quickly made it another block to my apartment where I had some packages made up. I'll have to remember to always have a package or two with me. Werewolf was excited with his treats, and she was happy to see the twenty-dollar bill. I was happy to be of service.

Facebook, December 5, 2015
Cleo and Sophia are ready for the holidays, and they have several outfits to show their holiday spirit! Of course, this is a different week same thing...went in for poop bags came out with sweaters, dresses, and Santa hats! I don't seem to be getting any better...

17

Christmas in SoCal

Facebook, December 25, 2015
It took a little convincing to get Cleo and Sophie to pose while they were napping on the balcony, but we finally got a nice Christmas picture 😊*.*
Merry Christmas everyone!!!

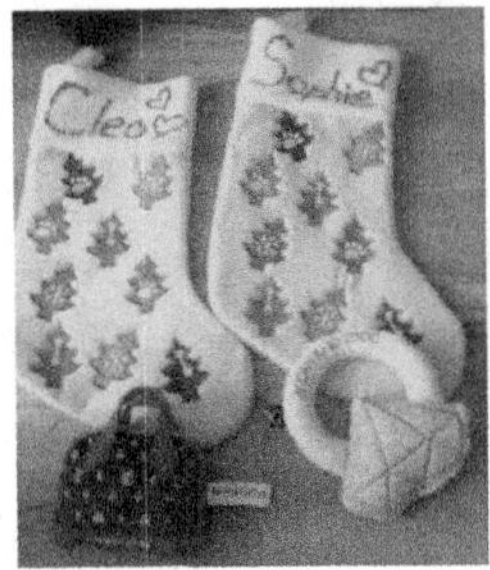

Facebook, December 25, 2015
Two of Cleo and Sophie's stocking stuffers.
The rest are already covered in drool thus not
making it into the pic.

I think I've become the cray-cray dog lady, but I don't care. I love my babies, and nothing nor no one comes before them.

I'm starting to get excited about spending the evening with Sarah, the Navy Fellow. She invited me to her place for dinner, which was very thoughtful. She too intrigues me like Tammy, a Navy person who meditates and can explain the different chakras. I know it is no accident that we are all here together and that I am learning so much from these ladies.

As I grab my phone and purse, I see I have a new text message from Dan. I haven't heard from him since his birthday. I open it to see it's a dancing cartoon lady. The song is from the '50s and is about missing someone on Christmas. I can feel the smile emerging across my face. I reply:

Thanks for brightening my day ☺

I throw my phone in my purse and check myself one last time in the bathroom mirror.

"Okay, girls, I won't be gone long. See you in a little bit! Love you!"

As I walk the six blocks to Sarah's place, I can feel myself beaming on the inside. He misses me! This is nice to know, but also not good for my desire to move on. After all, I just did the hypnotherapy a couple of months ago. Will this set me back, just being happy to hear from him? Am I already spiraling down because I texted him back? Surely not. I mean, the point of the session was for me to be more empowered, to love myself and to ensure that I am looking out for all those little Avas who are still a part of me. So, if I don't allow this to spiral out of control, I am good right?

Over the years, I had done my work – or so I thought. I'd been doing my work since the early days of Iyanla Vanzant on the Oprah Winfrey Show. I've been in the *Meantime* several times I've been from the basement to the attic and back to the one of the middle floors. My soul has *Opened Up* and I have cried many *Yesterdays*. But even with all those books, having read them several times, and even after reading many other self-help books, I wasn't able to realize that the core of the problem lies in the fact that I just did not love myself – didn't value myself. I knew my self-esteem was low, but I couldn't read these books and reach to the root of the problem. But, boy, I could quote them! Quote them and pass them along to others for their healing. I was so lost, but because I'd read these books, was going to therapy, and could identify the brokenness in others, I thought I was in a better place.

It wasn't until I experienced Affect Bridge hypnotherapy that my soul truly did open. This powerful technique allowed me to travel back to my youth and comfort all my younger selves. I vowed to honor them and protect them, as they are still within me as an adult. Knowing I have this responsibility to take care of all the little Avas immediately empowered me to walk away, to not be wrapped up in Dan. I was able to stay in a hotel a block away from his place when I was back in D.C. the other month and not have any temptation to talk to him or see him.

I know there is still more work to do, but I will not worry about it; just let it be what it will be. I'm now at Sarah's front door. I'm only going to be in this moment and not bring Dan to Christmas dinner.

Facebook, December 31, 2015
I was blessed to spend this last day of 2015 with this as my view. I stopped after having walked for a few hours thinking, reflecting, and thanking God for a fabulous year! If I went into all the great blessings of this year and the great blessings He's already shown me for 2016 this post would turn into a dissertation so I will just say 2015 has been fabulous and 2016 is going to be absolutely amazing!!!

Also, I want to say thanks to all of you for your kind and well wishes during my journey across the country and I am very thankful for everyone who is now a part of my life here. All of you have been part of God's plan to take me to the next level in my life. I am truly blessed!

I've spent many a New Year's Eve alone – usually going to bed before midnight, but this year I don't feel alone. I always felt lonely on New Year's Eve, even the few years when I was in a relationship. Even those years where there was a man, he was an ass, and so there was never excitement about what the new year would bring for us as a couple. Today there is a shift. Today I feel I am with myself. Sounds odds to say, but I feel complete. I complete me. Me and my little Avas. We're good.

18

New Year, New Me

Facebook, January 1, 2016
"When you're in your own lane there is no traffic."
We were all brought to this earth to fulfill a unique divine purpose.
When we are in tune with that purpose we accomplish so much and give
so much to others.

I love this quote. I have a purpose: to write. Lately, when I see children, I smile, and I am filled with such delight. They laugh, they giggle, some of them even cry. They ask way too many questions about all the uniqueness of this life. They reach and grab, they touch things. They try to understand, they try to figure things out, but all with a sense of ease – no frustration, no hurry. They're simply curious and loving and embracing life with a lovely inquisitive spirit. When I see children, I can feel the smile on my face and the twinkle in my eyes. I see the innocence of a child who has no clue what they'll be when they grow up but has all the possibilities in the world. Then, I think of myself – that seven-year-old who wrote that book and took it to school, whose teacher laminated it, bound it with yarn, let me read it to the class, and then added it to the reading nook in our classroom. I still think of my book nestled between Dr. Seuss' *The Cat in the Hat* and the many tales of *Curious George*. My book, the book I wrote. So, yeah, I've been a published author since age seven. Thinking of it this way feels good, but I long to have the endless possibilities back. At seven, I came home, wrote, and illustrated a book – and not once during that evening did I stop and think, "What if no one likes it?" or, "Why am I doing this and not something more acceptable?" I was a little girl who played alone most of the time, read a lot of books, and one day knew I wanted to author a book, so I did. I want to find that little girl again. Yes, I've visited all my little Avas and I'm protecting them now, but maybe I need to let go and let their innocence inspire me.

I authored a book at seven, dreamed of being a nurse until age ten when I saw a soldier who had his kneecap blown off in the emergency room one night, and by the time I was sixteen wanted to be a fashion buyer and only thought of living in New York in some cute brownstone – long before there was a *Sex and the City*. That little girl got older, got to college, got scared, didn't major in marketing as she was advised to do so by a fashion buyer, but changed her major to accounting, fearful that she wouldn't succeed – and so desperate to get out of her parents' control.

In a way, I guess I did march out there and I got my freedom the only way I knew how. Yes, many of my instructors told me to major in English, but I couldn't see where that would get me. I didn't want to be a teacher, and it didn't seem like majoring in English was the right thing. No one told me I could be a book editor. No one told me about journalism. I guess I should've known these things or done the research to know, but I was naïve, and I knew business. I knew my older sister had majored in marketing, and all I wanted was not to return to my parents' house after graduation. I knew an accounting degree would yield a decent job and good salary, so I got my freedom – but I really didn't. Now it's time to really get that freedom. My restitution!

For years, I've had the same argument with my father about my writing. I'm not exactly sure why we continue to go back and forth. I did listen to him ten years ago and stopped writing all together, stopped taking writing classes, and tried to focus on this ridiculous career that I hate. I was so resentful, yet I kept going. I kept doing everything that everyone told me to do, now here I am – not where I want to be, but no longer too scared to just walk away and live off my savings. I will succeed this time. I know that I'll make it. I don't care what they think anymore.

It's not a drive to prove them wrong, it's a drive to finally be what God placed me on this earth to be – to be in my lane, the right lane, as a writer who educates, inspires, and entertains. He's told me this before and He's made it clear I do not have a choice in this. I don't know why I keep arguing with my father about this. I don't know why I care that my mother shrugs her shoulders or laughs at me. I don't know why I let them put all kinds of doubt in my head. They don't know any better – all they know is to hold on to every dollar they have. All they know is there may not be anything tomorrow. I wasn't raised this way, so I don't know this way. What I know is they say that Generation X people will change jobs seven times in their lifetime before they retire, and I still have the same job that I've had for twenty years. I'm blessed because it pays well and blessed because it's leading me to this writing career by way of this fellowship. I'm not unaware of how I got here. I'm not unaware that I had to take certain classes to be qualified for this fellowship, to get this opportunity, to be in California for a year, to meet all these wonderful, fabulous people, to be inspired to write again. I totally understand all of this, and I have nothing but gratitude, but I can no longer maintain the status quo of self-imprisonment at Shawshank.

Facebook, January 1, 2016
Iyanla Vanzant on Twitter
"Move toward your wildest dream, take the labels off your mind, and step boldly into your greatness."

And so, I have. I write – again. I've even enrolled in a writing workshop at Santa Monica Community College. I am excited for this experience. I once enrolled in a similar class in Arlington the first year I moved to the area. The first night, each student was asked to read a few pages of a story they were working on.

I was so nervous about reading that I never looked up and when I finally did the class was looking at me in awe and the instructor began praising my work. I guess the story was captivating. I dropped out of the class after the first week. I had gone back and forth with my dad about writing again and I allowed the doubt to settle into the point of quitting. This time there's no quitting!

Each morning, I begin the day with ease. I walk the dogs, then sit quietly for my morning mediation. I've converted the slender space along the side of the bed into my meditation place. I feel secure sitting in about three feet of space and looking out at my ocean view before I close my eyes. Upon opening them, there it is – the tiny blip of a view that was promised to me when I requested this unit. It brings a smile to my face. I've managed to nuzzle in a vision board against the window. It's small enough not to block the ocean view, and just large enough to fill with my hopes and dreams (including a quaint Spanish-style house in Beverly Hills). I am dreaming big this year!

Yes, this is possible. A writing career, a big, beautiful home and living free!

Facebook, January 8, 2016
I'll be live streaming this since I'm not in the DMV this year but wanted to share for those who are. Bishop Jakes brings it every year!!! I always leave more charged up and ready to hit the year running!

Love this yearly revival! Marva invited us a few years ago, and the crew has been going ever since. I'm sure they are there now, having rode together, joking and laughing up I-495. Every year, Bishop Jakes seems to say something hopeful that only I heard. The ensuing conversation typically goes something like, "Wow, I can't believe how Bishop Jakes said we're not mistakes. God has a plan for us."

"Really, when did he say that?"

"Right at the beginning, right after the prayer."

"I missed that. Did you hear that, Terry?"

"No, Marva, I didn't but glad you got your message, Ava!"

I know God will allow us to hear or see things that others may not, and I'm fine with it. I've now come to expect it, and I don't bat an eye. It can occur at any time, and it always happens at revival night at First Baptist Church of Maryland.

I am getting a little sad that I am not there, and sad that I've been out here six months having barely spoken to any of the crew. I should reach out, but there's a part of me that just doesn't want to – a part of me that's being selfish (or self-loving) and soaking up every moment of this time out here. Sheryl said they understood, and I believe this to be true. I really do love it here, and I hope I am able to find a job after the fellowship. This place has revived me in so many ways and opened parts of my soul. Some people travel to foreign countries and have spiritual awakenings. For me, my awakening is occurring in Southern California.

Facebook, January 8, 2016
Happy birthday to you! Happy birthday to you! Happy birthday dear Sophie! Happy birthday to you 🐾🎉💕🎂. Today my little girl is 10 years old!

These doggy pastries are adorable! Better than anything I've purchased in the DMV – but of course they would be. These L.A. folks love their dogs! I got these at the famers market at the Grove. I must admit I've been dying to get out there. I've heard about it for years, and it's only fitting to place my feet on such sacred ground. I haven't been as touristy as I thought I would be. Yes, I had to take the drive down Rodeo Drive and see the famous "Pretty Woman" hotel, and since I was in Beverly Hills I had to drive down several of the streets and gawk at the houses, but mainly I've been nestled in Santa Monica, Earthing with Cleo, and Sophie in the park each day and writing in the evenings. Even work doesn't feel like work. I go, make progress on my research paper, support other research with the Big Brains Fellows, and then I come home. No stress, no taskers, no Col. Baker weirdness, no wheels up threats. It's been blissful.

Facebook, January 8, 2016
T.D. Jakes on Twitter
"You cannot grow until you become frustrated with where you are! Exposure will make you move forward! #JointRevival @FBCG @GMCHC"

Amen!!! Preach it, Bishop Jakes! I may not be there live and in person this year, but I can get the message just the same via Twitter!

Facebook, January 17, 2016 – San Diego
You know the saying you make plans and God laughs. Well, we were living proof of that this weekend but as always God's plans always out rank mine ☺ I didn't do one thing I planned to do but the blessings I received were 1000 times better than any activity I could have done this weekend!

The two-hour drive from Santa Monica to San Diego took almost five, and I missed seeing Joel Osteen – the only reason the girls and I drove down here this weekend. But, as always, God is the bomb! I checked into the resort, ordered room service, fed the dogs, and started writing. I'm working on my edits from the class feedback from my writing class and I'm flowing like a river!

The class instructor has provided great critiques for my novel and also very encouraging motivation for completing it. The other students in the class are a joy to be with every week. Everyone has their unique writing style, and we all are writing in different genres which makes for great entertainment when we read our work to the class each week.

A while back I started working on this novel, the one I know will turn into a Hallmark movie or maybe even a miniseries. The genre is historical fiction, and it tells the story of one of my great aunts who lived in Newark, New Jersey. She and some of her siblings moved there during the great migration in 1945. They too were searching for their freedom. They were escaping the harsh cruelty of the south. My aunt was married several times and I am curious as to why. I never asked her and now she is gone so I can't. But, I can imagine how, and I think it's rooted in her issues with self-love. I write as though I were her. How could I have married so many times, who were these men and what attracted me to them? What I enjoy about my writing process is I have no clue what I am writing as I am typing. It's a strange occurrence. I just sit down and start typing without the standard outline and character development process first being completed. It is as if the story is being told to me and I am in suspense as to what's going to happen next. I wonder if it is being told to me. What if my aunt is writing this story through me?

Facebook, February 2, 2016 –

Gorgeous day for lunch outside! Fried ice cream food truck!

Big Brains does not require much of us Fellows, but they do highly encourage our weekly lunch outing. What a requirement, huh? Oh, poor us, find a place to have lunch in Santa Monica once a week. Honestly, though, it really was rough at first, and not just the lunches but the entire fellowship. With all of us military and civilians used to structure, having a fellowship at a place like Big Brains was nerve racking for us. We are set free for a year to research whatever we want and there's no one to report to daily. Our research paper is only twenty pages, and we get a year to write it. And then there's the casual dress code that took me a good month to master. Now I show up in my jeans and Chuck Taylors and feel just as smart as I did in my tailored suit and four-inch heels at Shawshank.

Sometimes it feels surreal that I am even here, but I do know that this is indeed a blessing that I will cherish forever.

Facebook, February 2, 2016
Ok Jill and Tammy it's here! Got my package today! My first 5K! So excited!

Tammy has convinced us to go to Temecula to participate in a 5K race over Valentine's Day weekend. Seeing as my birthday is just a few days before Valentine's, and I've never participated in a race before, it seemed like a promising idea to try something new. Plus, Temecula is known for its vineyards, so why not?

I've been running since I got here, and I've clocked myself going further than 5K, so this should be a breeze. I see myself floating through the vineyard effortlessly and smiling – moving with the grace of a 5K Goddess!

Since it's also my birthday week, I've booked a huge suite for myself. Also, Jill, Tammy, and I made appointments at the resort's spa. I'm looking forward to this experience. There hasn't been one thing so far that I have not enjoyed – from the big chop of my hair, to energy healing and hypnosis, to learning to meditate, to this writing class and all the wonderment in between. I deserve every aspect of this life. Every experience is mine to love, to embrace and to slowly set me free.

Facebook, February 3, 2016
It just got real! Just purchased my own shoes -no more renting that's how much I'm loving my spin class!!!

Who would have thought I'd love a spin class that takes place in a dark room with the instructor yelling out motivational quotes for the hour, but I indeed love it and I'm shaping up nicely. Between my mediation and exercise, I am becoming a whole new person. I really do want to take more swim lessons, as well. The six classes were great and helped me gain some confidence, and at the end the instructor did say he'd trust me to be in pool alone, so I take that as great advancement in my abilities. However, I want to go deeper, to really be transcending on the water as I do when I meditate. Being in the water was a liberating experience. I struggled the first few weeks but then the instructor gave me the best advice which was to just Zen out. I thought of it as though I was meditating, and I closed my eyes and let go. God is everywhere and He's in the pool in Culver City. This is no different than being a part of the Universe, and this can't hurt me. I just have to allow myself to be present and trust. God is in me, and so there is nothing to fear. My lessons became much easier after that, and I ended my last lesson doing twenty laps in the shallow end. Not bad for having not swam in nearly thirty years!

Facebook, February 6, 2016
This morning's meditation spot.
Scenic fuel for today's 5K!

19

Ready to Run!

We arrived in Temecula late yesterday evening and had a wonderful dinner. This morning, as I open the French doors to the balcony, I am filled with a calm energy. I would have thought I'd be freaking out as this is my first race, but nope. I'm standing here overlooking a vineyard and, in the distance, I see beautiful mountains that show a hint of snow. How is this even possible? I'm in Southern California, staying at a fancy resort, about to run in a race, and starting off my day with meditation. My, how my life has changed! This time last year, I was preparing for foot surgery alone and working towards moving out here. Never in a million years would I have thought I'd accomplish so much and be in such a better headspace.

Lesson learned – running on the beach trail at 7 PM is NOT the same as running through a hilly vineyard at 9 AM under the hot California sun! I almost quit, but Jill was so wonderful and wouldn't let me give up. She was so close to crossing the finish line, but then turned around and trotted over it with me. What a wonderful soul!

Now it's time for dinner and a lot of drinking! Mind you, we had our fill yesterday at the resort, as we did plenty of wine tasting with a guy who didn't bother to cut us off after our five-limit punch card. Tammy, the true runner of us three, is ready to celebrate, as she finished the race in under eight minutes. I have no idea when Jill and

I crossed the finish line, but I do know we found Tammy looking very rested and sipping on a glass of wine as she waited for us.

Facebook, February 11, 2016
Enjoying a fabulous day off work!!! Oh, and the waffle is ok 'cause I kicked butt in my spin class last night 😄

Today, I'm on a beach. Last year, I was laid up post-surgery on my birthday. I am at Redondo Beach on this beautiful day, looking out at the ocean with the boats far off the coast. My plan was to come here today, grab some breakfast, hit the beach, and just chill. That's exactly what I am doing.

My dark green cargo pants are pulled up to my knees and my Chuck Taylors are in my hands as I walk along the edge of the water. I feel like a little child. I giggle every time the water rushes up and splashes hard against my body. Seeing how wet I am from my white silk blouse to my pants, the idea of rolling up my pants feels insignificant at this point. There is just a handful of people around, and that makes this all the better. Man, to spend my birthday at the beach…and I didn't have to book a vacation to do it! God, please help me to stay here after this fellowship. I want to stay here forever! There's nothing for me back in the DMV. There's no Dan, even though he has been calling again. I know it'll never lead to anything. I hate that building, that prison, that Shawshank.

I know getting a job here will be different from my fellowship at Big Brains. I realize I'll be back to a more rigid schedule, but it will be one hundred percent worth it to have this life in the evenings and on the weekends. I've been applying for jobs for a while now, but so far nothing. I am even willing to leave the federal government and have applied for a handful of private sector positions — including production studios, as advised by my personal trainer. His thought was that if I want to be in the industry as a writer whose novels turn into movies, why not get my foot in the door with my B.S. in accounting and my MBA? It made plenty of sense to me, but nothing has come of it so far. However, it's only February and my fellowship doesn't end until June, so I've got plenty of time.

Facebook, February 17, 2016
It's raining! Guess we're going to have to wear our new raincoats!!!

I got these adorable raincoats from the pet boutique in North Hollywood. I ran across it during the holidays when I was looking for bows for the girls to match their Christmas dresses. While there, I met the owner and we talked for a while. I shared with him I, too, had dog business back in D.C., and we exchanged information. He and his partner were gracious and donated a few bags of treats to my homeless dog campaign, and they even discussed working with them in their business, but I've not heard back from them. Prior to this enlightened awakening I'm having, I would have thought them to be fake, just talking. Now I know I am not ready for such a thing, so my energy is keeping them away. I can daydream all I want about leaving my government job but there's still a sense of uncertainty about it. I do hope I can get on the other side of this uncertainty soon.

Facebook, February 27, 2016
Excited to see Deepak Chopra and Eckhart Tolle with the girls!

I really can't believe I am about see these two remarkable people. I was introduced to both via the Oprah Winfrey Show and now I will be in the same room with them. I am currently taking Deepak's Synchrodestiny course online and it is changing my life. Sarah told me about this course, and I am grateful she did. Every day, I learn a little more about being open to receiving and achieving a higher state of consciousness, and every day something new and wonderful happens to move me closer to making my writing career a real thing – like finding out about a class being taught out in the Valley in a few weeks by a talent agent, and a two-day class for writers with a panel of Hollywood agents, directors, and producers. My vibe is more than I can describe with words. I think the best way to describe it is liberated!

While I am excited to be here, I am giving up the opportunity to see Iyanla Vanzant at Michael Beckwith's Agape church tonight. I was thrilled when I learned she was coming and I purchased my ticket immediately, not realizing this event conflicted with seeing her. The good news is my hairdresser is going in my place, so I think that's why I purchased the ticket in the first place – to give it to her, even though I really thought it was for me at the time.

My hairdresser here is nothing like Monique. She carries herself with such a peacefulness that I sometimes think she is floating around her salon suite. She, like my personal trainer, is somewhat of a muse for me. In either case, Shelly will be at Agape tonight, and based on what she's shared with me, I believe the Universe orchestrated my double-booking for tonight. Synchrodestiny! I am though looking forward to hearing all about it from Shelly. Iyanla always brings the truth!

Facebook, March 6, 2016
Los Angeles Valley College
Attending a seminar on how to move forward with all my writing projects! In just the last week God has brought so many wonderful people into my life to make it happen!

I am in a room filled with anticipation and hope. The faces are inviting, and there is a sense of knowing with each of them. Their ages range from early twenties to late sixties. There's no stopping a dream when it's inside you!

The talent agent giving the presentation today has worked with many of the greats, including Aaron Spelling! He appears to be in his fifties, with long dark brown hair. He's noticeably arrogant, and he's wearing a black leather jacket although it's hot as hell in the Valley! I've heard this over the years: it must be at least ten degrees hotter here than in Santa Monica. Who would think a few miles away from the ocean would bring desert heat?

Mickey, the talent agent, has given a great presentation, and surprisingly there are not a lot of people hanging around asking questions. I take the opportunity to introduce myself.

"Hello, thank you for a great overview of the business."

"You're quite welcome. What's your itch?"

"My itch?"

"Yeah, your thing that you want to be known for?"

"Oh, I am a writer."

"You looking to write for television?"

"No, I want to write novels and children's books, but I'm hopeful they will be turned into movies and television shows."

"Great expectation. This is becoming the thing, you know. Not so much original movie scripts, as movie producers are finding remarkable stories in books – and many from unknown authors."

"Oh, yes, I've heard about something like that." I stop before saying more, as I can tell I need to play into his sense of all-knowing.

"If you ever want a consultation, let me know."

"As a matter of fact, I would. I'll connect with you via email?"

"Yep, sounds great. Nice meeting you…"

"Ava, my name is Ava."

"Great, yeah, Ava, let's connect."

And just like that, I'm about to have a consultation with a Hollywood agent!

Facebook, March 14, 2016

Took the afternoon off for a meeting that got rescheduled so...since I'm here in lovely Studio City might as well have lunch and bottomless mimosas ☺. Stay tuned for tomorrow's post..."The Rescheduled Meeting" So excited about it but want to wait to share what it's about until it happens. But I will say this, God BLESSES ALL THE TIME!!! All you have do is have the intention.

Facebook, March 15, 2016

Studio City

The rescheduled meeting is about to occur! Today I am meeting with a talent agent who used to be the agent for Aaron Spelling! In case you don't recall the name...he was a mega hit producer of shows like 90201, Charlie's Angels, The Love Boat, Dynasty and Charmed to name a few!

We are going to discuss my transition into my writing career, and I am so thankful and blessed to have met him and have this amazing opportunity! GOD DOES IT ALL THE TIME!!! Have the intention and faith and everything is possible!

God's plans for me to come out to California were so much better than I could have ever imagined. He opened me up to accept the gift He has given me and is opening all these beautiful doors of opportunity so I can move into my true purpose!

The advice I am receiving from Mickey is extremely helpful. Just meeting with an agent makes me feel like I am part of the "Industry." Sitting in the café, watching him wave as someone walks by, he tells me was the producer of the show *Designing Women*. He says, "Just the other day, when I was talking to Magic..." Silly, I know, but it fuels my motivation. I can be a part of this world, and I am open to all it has to offer!

Facebook, March 18, 2016
Holistic Spa
Okay, Tammy and Jill, it's time for me to try the "you-know-what."

The "you-know-what" would be a V-Steam, and I loved it! Who would have thought steamed tea up your vajayay would feel so good! I also enjoyed the whirlpool, salt room and infrared rooms. I can get use to this place. I've been to spas before, but this is a holistic haven. The V-Steam is absolutely wonderful! I saw it on Tia and Tamara Mowry's reality show a couple of years ago, and made a note that, should I ever make it to the L.A. area, I'd try it. Well, here I am, and at the very spa they went to. I am certain my ass is occupying one of the seats they sat on! Yeah, that's weird, but I'm a fan of theirs! And I am not a hundred percent sure, but I think I had a brief conversation with someone famous – but I couldn't quite place her face. She was coming out of the infrared room. She was so pleasant and told me I'd thoroughly enjoy the experience, and she was right. Sitting there in that room, sweating out toxins, was like being transported to another realm. I was in there alone, which made the experience even more sacred. The heat lifted my mind, body, and soul to a new level of purity.

Facebook, March 31, 2016
Chilling in the park with my lil babies.

I'm hanging with the girls and giving them extra mommy-time before I make a quick trip back to the DMV to get my taxes done. I know it's crazy that I feel the need to fly back for this, as if I have some super-powered accountant when all I do is go to a local business that I've gone to for years. But Steve is the only person I trust.

Plus, Dan wants to spend time together this weekend. I still have my guard up, as I am big momma Ava to all my little Avas, but I must admit that I am extremely curious as to why he has reappeared and now wants to spend time with me. We haven't spoken much since his dancing Christmas cartoon, but the conversations have been good. We're back to our norm.

I love that about us. No matter how we part ways, whenever we reunite, we don't miss a beat. We are good friends at the core. I must believe that's what keeps us close, despite the fact the romantic aspect always goes to shit. Anyway, he wants to pick me up from the airport and has offered for me to take a nap at his place since I'm flying in on the red-eye and my hotel room won't be ready for several hours after I land. Afterwards, he's offered to drive me around to a few places where I need to file some paperwork for my dog business. This is something I love about him. Sometimes he is thoughtful and loving. But then his actions (and my reactions to those actions) always freak the shit out of him, and he shuts down and walks away. I am trying to hold positive thoughts that this time will be different, but something in my gut is telling me it will not be.

20

The Metro

They say to trust your gut, and I get the feeling now is a good time to do this. I am not sure why, but something feels off. I started having this feeling about twenty minutes before the plane landed. I'm exiting the jetway and texting Dan. I look for the nearest restroom and go inside. As I close the door to the stall and move to place my phone in my purse, I see Dan's reply:

On my way.

Seems like he would already be here but perhaps he got caught up with something and lost track of time.

As I exit the restroom, I take my phone out of my purse and see another text from Dan:

Traffic is horrible. Summit with the president. Taking the Metro instead. Meet me on the southbound side.

Okay, Dan does live just a few blocks from the White House, so if the president is part of this summit traffic would suck today. However, the southbound side is strange, considering he lives in D.C., but he is heading south to get here so I guess he wants me to meet him when he arrives though it would make more sense for him to exit the train and then find his way to the northbound side since that's the direction we are going.

I begin walking through the airport and head out to the Metro. There is a train pulling up as I make it to the platform. As the doors open, I look up and down the platform and spot Dan existing one of the cars. He is freaking out. I can see it on his face. After all these years it's easy to see. It's in his eyes. He looks like someone is robbing him at gunpoint or just jumped out of a closet and yelled, "boo."

"Hello, Ava." (What? No "Ava-Flava"?)

"Hi. Traffic's bad today?"

We give each other a hug. He stands back to check me out. I'm dressed up in my SoCal style, with my dark green cargo pants from Anthropologie and off-the-shoulder oversized blouse. I'm standing in three-inch open-toed Stewart Weitzman ankle boots. Most shocking to him, I'm sure, is that my hair is in its natural state – three inches of massive, tight coils, colored a light brown and adorning my head like Nefertiti's crown. Many heads were turning at LAX, JFK and DCA. I'm feeling like the Klymaxx song, "The Men All Pause." But the look on Dan's face is one of bewilderment.

"Yeah, it's bad. I figured I'd get down here a lot quicker by taking the train."

"Makes sense. Don't we need to get to the other side?"

"Why?"

"I thought we were going to your place so I could take a nap?"

"Oh, yeah, well, why don't you call and see if your room is ready first since we are just two stops away."

"Okay."

I pull out my phone and dial the hotel. As I do, the train pulls up. Dan grabs my suitcase and quickly moves inside. Damn, I guess he wants to get rid of me already. I am informed that the rooms are not yet ready, but they will put me on the waitlist. There is a possibility I can check in prior to 3 PM. I hang up the phone and tell this to Dan.

"You know, they'll probably have something ready by the time we get there."

"Maybe, but we're only ten minutes away."

"You never know. Stay positive."

"Right."

What the hell? Why in the hell did this man say he wanted to see me, only to hurriedly get me to my hotel – nowhere near his place? Why am I asking why? I knew damn well that offering to nap in his bed was way more of a commitment than he could handle. Now he's freaking out. Oh well, there's nothing I can do about it now but go with the flow.

Upon our arrival at the hotel, I check in with the front desk. Just my luck, they have a room ready for me. We head up and I am remarkably calm. The pre-meditative me would have been all over his ass about this weirdness, but I'm noticing I'm not really moved by it at all. I had a "what the hell" moment back on the train, and now I'm just whatever about it.

I open the door and excuse myself to the restroom. I check myself out in the mirror. Yep, I look so damn hot! Nothing to do but go out here and see how this story unfolds.

"I can't believe I haven't seen you in almost a year."

"Time has flown by really quickly. You still liking it out there? A few months ago, you were ready to move there permanently."

"Yep, I've applied for over a one hundred jobs. I'm hopeful one of them will come through."

"I'm sure that will be the case."

"Thanks for your advice on where to live after the fellowship, and the encouragement to go ahead and buy a place now."

In one of our conversations a few weeks prior, Dan said I should just go ahead and buy a place. It would surely guarantee I'd find a job. I must hand it to him: he beams far more positive energy and manifestation than I do.

"No problem. Just makes sense to me to do that."

We are both sitting on the edge of the bed. This small talk is awkward. Granted, it's conversation we'd normally have, but in the air hangs a stench of "I'm about to fuck you over with my commitment phobia bullshit." I'm thinking: "It's been almost a year since I've had sex. We are here, why not fuck?" Shit, I'm horny and I've just begun to enter the dating world again. I may not have purchased a home out there yet, but I'm sending positive vibes by joining dating sites and getting to know men from the area. I'm currently really intrigued by an Asian artist who lives in Hollywood. We've only texted a few times, but I love his free-spirited nature. I think dating him would be a profound change from the stuffy DMV-types I've been around all these years (including Dan). But the Artsy Asian is not here, Dan is.

I don't wait for any signs from Dan, I simply turn to face him more directly and begin to unbutton his shirt.

"Oh, so you got me in this room to seduce me?"

"Hey, I was trying to take a nap, but that plan changed."

We are an inch away from each other's lips as he slips off his shirt. I reach for his belt, and he raises his arm to let me unbuckle it. As he stands to slide down his jeans, I slip my blouse off and he walks behind me and unfastens my bra. His fingers are lightly stroking my nipples, which begin to harden. He turns me around and unties the string on my pants, sliding both my panties and pants down. Standing there staring at each other, we begin a long passionate kiss. He slowly lowers me to the bed, unties my boots, and in one quick motion slides my panties, pants, and boots off. He steps out of his jeans and straddles me on the bed.

As we kiss, my hands find their way to his boxers, and I pull at them. They lower enough for his length to emerge. He moves to remove his boxers and positions himself on his knees on the bed. I know what he wants, and I devour him completely. As I pleasure him, his moans become louder and louder until he pulls out of my mouth and motions for me to turn around. He enters me from behind with a deep thrust. I gasp for a moment, as it's been a while since anything other than a tampon has been inside me. Then I relax. Instantly, we are in a delightful rhythm. He's stroking and I'm bouncing back on him. Repeatedly our bodies meet, and I can feel my body getting hotter and hotter. Damn, I've missed this! He pulls out, flips me over, and enters me again. He's not a missionary position guy, but today he is on top and thrusting hard and slow. I meet each thrust with a raising and swirl of my hips. I can't believe how great our sexual chemistry has been since I've been stuck in right brain mode. How can I live without this? How can anyone live without the pleasures of sex? As we reach our climaxes, he slowly lowers his body on mine and kisses my neck, then my lips.

"You're a wild woman, Ava," he says as he pulls out of me curls up next to me. I love spooning with him.

"Me? Oh no, you're the wild one!"

As I laugh, he pulls me closer.

"I'll call it a tie!"

We are both quiet for a long time, naked and spooning. There is a peace I have with this man, even after all the shit we've put each other through.

"I'd better get going."

"I thought we were spending the day together?"

"Change of plans."

"Oh?"

Dan has gotten out of bed and is getting dressed. I'm sitting in the middle of the bed, naked.

"Yeah, sorry about that. So, what are your plans for the rest of the day?"

"That's unfortunate. I've got to file some paperwork in D.C., and then meet my tax guy at six. What about you?"

I don't bother to ask about Dan being my personal driver for the day. I know this is no longer on the table.

"I have a condo to show this afternoon, and I need to study to take the Maryland real estate exam. I want to be licensed across the DMV. After Maryland, I'll get my license in Virginia."

"That's cool. I'm really happy for you, for going after what you wanted."

"Thanks."

I move to get dressed, and as I do, I ponder taking a shower first, but decide I don't give a fuck and just put on the clothes I traveled in. As I do, I'm looking at Dan looking at me.

"What are you looking at?"

"Nothing. You. You really like it out there?"

"Yes, I really do. Is that crazy?"

"No, not at all. I love L.A. I'd move there myself, but I have a lot of connections out here and if I'm going to have a go at real estate then I need to stay here for a while."

"Makes sense."

"Yeah, it does. I'll come back after you get your taxes done and we can have dinner."

"Okay."

We walk to the door, and he turns to me. He leans over and gives me a kiss on the forehead. I'm flattered by the forehead kiss. It's sweet and gentle.

"I'll see you a few hours."

"Okay, I hope your showing goes well."

"Thanks."

He smiles as he turns to leave. I close the door.

I guess maybe I was wrong about him freaking out. I think, though, he is a little freaked – hence not going to his place nor driving me around this afternoon. But he's not too freaked out that he just didn't show up or told me we can only be friends. But then again, we are only "just friends," friends who fuck on occasion versus on a weekly basis.

I don't know, and, again, I'm not going to put any thought into it. I just had amazing sex after nine months, so at least there's that.

Feeling carefree and whimsical, I decide to blow off filing the paperwork, convincing myself I can do it online when I return to California. Instead, I head down to the Potomac River. It's April, but it's unusually warm for this time of year.

Facebook, April 1, 2016

So, here's something funny. I lived in the D.C. area for eight years and lived a mile from Old Town Alexandria for most of those years and spent many a day shopping and spa hoping just a block or two away but today while here for a super short trip was the first day that I saw the Potomac from Old Town! I'm usually on the other side of the Woodrow Wilson bridge hanging out at the National Harbor! And... The first time I rode the Old Town trolley how crazy is this???!!!

Today has been splendid! Yeah, it started out a little strange, but it's ending rather nicely. Taxes are done, and I'm heading back to the hotel to meet up with Dan.

I get back to my room, take a shower and change. I'm wearing a simple black strapless maxi dress with a coral sweater and black sandals. I check my phone to see if Dan has called, but there's nothing. I send him a text to see when he will arrive, as I am starving, and he writes back immediately:

Hey, sorry still studying. Go ahead and have dinner without me. Be there by 9.

I text back an "okay" and head down to the restaurant in the hotel. No need to go out anywhere. This will do for tonight.

As I wait for my food, I do an internet search for "What does it mean when a man kisses you on the forehead?" The results are pretty much unanimous. It's a sign of genuine love and respect – something a father does to a daughter, or a friend does to his female friend. Okay, so it's not a terrible thing, and it aligns with where we are in our newfound relationship… well, except for the fucking earlier today.

I finish my meal and head upstairs. I'm exhausted. I never did take a nap today. I get undressed and climb into bed. I close my eyes to rest while I wait for Dan to arrive.

When I awake, I see light throughout the room. I look at my phone and see it's 7 AM. Wow, I must have been tired. I grab my phone again, now thinking Dan called and I missed him. I'd hate to think he came over last night and I didn't answer the phone. I look, and there are no missed calls. Interesting, but not shocking, since I know he wanted to study last night. I don't know why, but I feel so indifferent about him at this moment. It's as if I am now coming to accept that I don't love him and I'm beginning to wonder if I ever did? And I must ask myself if I've ever loved him or is this no different than my ex in Oklahoma? Did I just grab hold of a man because he was in my life and hope like hell he would give me the love and affection I never received as a child? Probably, most definitely yes. I mean why would Dan be any different. It's not like I'd evolved enough from therapy to avoid this approach when Dan and I first met.

Look at you Ava! This has got to the mediation! Oh, thank you God I am changing!

My thoughts are interrupted by my ringing phone. It's Dan.

"Hey. Good morning."

"Good morning. Did you get any sleep?"

"Yes, I did. I needed it. I've never taken a red-eye before. I didn't realize how tired I'd be.

"Yeah, they can wear you out."

"So how did your studying go?"

"It was good. So, listen, I have to tell you something."

"Okay."

"I need you to know that I don't love you. I don't love you, and I never have, and I will never be able to."

"You know, that's interesting because I was just thinking the same thing about you."

"Really?"

"Yeah. Pretty odd coincidence, huh?"

"I guess it is."

"Okay, well, thanks for letting me know. Do you want to stop by today to say goodbye?"

"No."

"Oh. Well, we may never see each other again. I could get one of those jobs in L.A. and I won't be coming back here."

"Yeah, I know."

"But we're friends?"

"Of course."

"So, as friends, we can't see each other and say goodbye? Have lunch, a quick hug or something?"

"No."

"Wow, well, okay. I guess this is goodbye then."

"Yes, it is."

"Okay, goodbye."

"Goodbye, Ava."

I know damn well this man didn't ask me to plan my tax trip around his schedule just to dump my ass like this. But then again, yes, he did. Yes, Ava, he does this all the fucking time. He just did this last July when you were out here for the orientation, and he did it in October when you were coming out to the Annual Leadership Conference. Oh, and he's done this shit for six damn years now!

I grab my phone and send off about twenty irate text messages to Dan. What the fuck? Okay. You had a moment, and now it's time to mediate.

I walk over to the armchair and have a seat. I open my phone to find my list of daily Sutras that I have now incorporated into my practice from Deepak Chopra's Synchodestiny course. It's Saturday and the Sutra is Ritam. "I am alert, awake to coincidences, and aware they are messages from God. I flow with the cosmic dance."

Well, the irony of today's sutra can't be lost on me. I did say it was quite the coincidence that I woke up thinking I didn't love Dan, and then he calls to tell me he doesn't love me either. But that's not why I got pissed. I got pissed because, as I said in one of my twenty text messages to him, he's a coward, and if he had any balls, he would have said it to my face. At least he would have been able to see me and say goodbye.

I need to meditate. I focus on the sutra and its associated affirmations and then I take a breath. I close my eyes and begin to meditate.

After my meditation, I hop in the shower. It was an exceptionally good mediation, and as I shower, I am reminded of a conversation I had with Nala a couple of weeks ago. I don't recall how we got on the subject of Dan, but I remember saying it would be okay if I never saw him again, that I knew my inner peace is easier to obtain without him in my life. I feel as though I was speaking from my heart and everything I said was true – or at least I believed it to be, but again I am confusing the issue. I'm disappointed that he doesn't want to see me, not that he doesn't love me. Maybe it's a control thing with me, I can see that being the case. I'm just not sure and I don't want to explore it right now. I came really close to letting those little Avas down and that can't happen. Oh, well.

Today is not as warm as yesterday, so I think I'll be inside – doing nothing because I didn't make any plans with my friends. I didn't tell them I was coming into town because I wanted to have the entire weekend with Dan. Yes, I will admit there was some hope that his wanting to spend the weekend with me meant he'd come around about us being in a committed relationship, that the truth he tells in his sleep would manifest into reality, but I guess not. I'm glad I kept my guard up, had some level of doubt. Or is that why things ended the way they did? Because I wasn't exuding enough positive energy? Again, who knows. I am in a very calm state, and I am not going to ruin it by overthinking things. Plus, I got laid, so there's some goodness in all of this. I'll head down for breakfast then spend the day writing. It'll be okay.

21

From Metro to Town Car

It's Sunday morning and I'm up early to catch my flight, so I'll have to mediate on the plane. I do love that about Vedic Meditation, you can do it anywhere. As I wait to check out at the front desk, I inform the bellhop I will need a cab. He nods and heads outside. Once I join him, he informs me he's having a challenging time getting cabs to the hotel and offers me a ride in the hotel's town car. I smile and say thank you and he takes my suitcase and loads it into the trunk. The driver opens the door and I climb inside. Oh, the irony. I arrived on the Metro but am heading back in a town car. This is most definitely a sign that things are going to get better from here on.

Facebook, April 10, 2016
What makes a good sibling? Someone who will be with you even on your not-so-great days. These are the best canine siblings I've ever known! Cleo had a small cyst removed from her eye and yes it was benign praise God!!! And Sophie has been super sweet to her big sister.

Back in SoCal and living life free of Dan has been great. I just wrapped up a two-day workshop with some of Hollywood's top directors, agents, and producers. The advice I received was phenomenal, including that I should make my first book about what I know. When I inquired as to what that is, I was reminded by one of the producers, to whom I introduced myself to as a Global Posture Strategist from the Pentagon who is out here working for Big Brains for a year. When I noted I had no intension of writing about anything that would land me in jail, or that would put me on CNN, he gave me a weird look.

"You don't tell the secrets. You tell us what you see. How it feels. That place is a mystery to most of the world, and you are someone who works there *and* writes – plus you are telling it from the angle of a civilian, not a military person. And as in every good story, you have a challenge: you want to be a writer fulltime – to make it your true profession. Tell that story. Add in the funny jokes you've shared with us about how your dad likes to brag that you work at the Pentagon and your rebuttal is, 'So does the guy that rings me up at McDonald's, and his mom probably brags to her friends about how her son works at the Pentagon.' The fact that there's a McDonalds in the place blows my mind!"

After the two days, I was convinced I should indeed write about my life at Shawshank, so I've put aside my other work and started writing about life in the building. I'm excited about it, with all the encouragement I received. I even got a "yes, I'd love to read it" response from several of the agents and producers when I sent them thank-you emails after the workshop. Eight years in that place. I should have this novel knocked out in no time.

In addition to the wonderful advice the two days spent in the heart of Hollywood was surreal. The workshop was a block away from the Hollywood Walk of Fame. Our lunch breaks allowed us to walk down Hollywood Boulevard and scout out a place to eat. Walking over the stars and reading the names, passing the Chinese Theatre, being here in this city, in this class, getting advice from people in the industry, encouraged to give my voice to something like Shawshank. Yes, this is real, and I deserve these moments!

Facebook, April 15, 2016
Mark Pierce Congrats!
Those in L.A. please support if you are able!

I met Mark during the two-day workshop. His indie film as received worldwide recognition, and I am greatly inspired by his motivation to stay the course. He is now debuting it here in L.A. and I will be there with bells on! I can't wait to arrive, looking elegant chic (not sure if that's a thing but...) After the workshop, I sent him a thank-you note and mentioned if he ever needed help with another film to please reach out. He wrote back and said he'd be happy to have my support. I am so sure I'll be living here after the fellowship that I am putting myself out there and networking. I may not buy a place,

appropriate to say it's a store that sells items primarily related to Hinduism. I am just learning about Hinduism mainly through the course with Deepak Chopra and it has led me to do more research. I now understand deities and how each holds special meaning and the support they provide.

Looking around I first see a large glass table. I approach it and I look down to see countless crystals! I'm in love! I brace myself knowing I will be spending a lot of time at this table and proceed to the back of the store where there are several large paintings on the wall. I see Ganesha, Shiva, Krishna, and others who I am not yet familiar with.

I turn to see a woman dressed in a red sari smiling at me.

"Oh, hello. I love these paintings. Do you have any that are a bit smaller than these?"

"Yes, of course, we have some gorgeous, embossed prints you may like."

"Do you have any of Ganesha and Krishna?"

"I am certain we do."

"She walks over to a bin and begins to flip through the prints."

"Here is a very nice one of Ganesha."

"Oh, it is lovely!"

The print is a beautiful gold with vibrant colors throughout. She hands me the print and continues flipping.

"Ah! And how lucky for you Krishna and Radha!"

"The print is remarkable, but I am not sure who Radha is?"

"Oh, my dear, Radha is Krishna's beloved. Together they represent the most perfect union."

"She doesn't need to say anymore as I am sold. I will read more about Radha this evening. I wonder how I missed learning about her before this moment?"

"Thank you. I will take both."

"Very well. Will that be all?"

"No, I would like to purchase some crystals as well. Would you be able to assist me?"

"Of course. What are you looking for?"

"I am not sure what crystal I need but something for overall support. I've been doing great with mediation, but I thought perhaps a crystal could also help. And a rose quartz."

"Sure."

"She walks back to the front stands on one side of the glass table. She opens the drawer and retrieves a tray of rose quartz crystals."

"Take a look dear. See which one wants to go home with you."

"Okay."

I understand that crystals have energy, and she says this like one of these is going to pick me verses the other way around. I stare at the tray and allow myself to relax. There is one tiny rose quartz that I am drawn to, so I pick it up. As I do I feel a tiny vibration in the palm of my hand where the stone is resting. You little one. You must be the one. I hold my hand out to the lady and she takes the crystal and places it in a small bag.

"Now, for something that will support you."

"Yes, please."

She moves to the left and opens another drawer. This time she is holding a tray of blue stones.

"This is Sodalite. I am hearing this is the best stone for you as it also supports building trust with yourself. I am hearing this is where your worry fear and doubt steam from."

I can't argue with her as it sounds correct to me. I am doing wonderfully with using all the new alternative healing methods I've learned but yes, I can't shake this sense that there's more I need to release. My desire to stay here and time running out with this fellowship does have me concerned even though I am doing my best to stay positive. Plus, I feel like there's more to staying here than I am currently understanding.

I stare at the tray but this time I am compelled to move my right hand over the tray. I feel a tingling sensation in my ring finger and stop immediately. I touch the stone that is right below my finger and hold it. This time there is not a vibrating sensation but there is heat. I hand this stone to the lady, and she smiles.

I feel good with my selections or maybe they selected me.

Facebook, May 22, 2016
World Dog Day West Hollywood

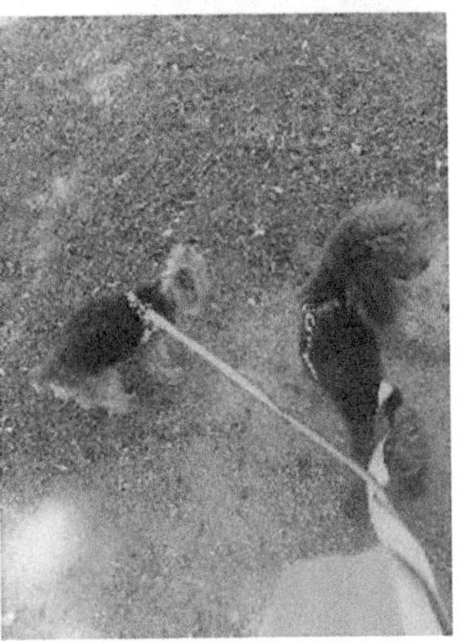

I had an exciting time today. It was nice to take the girls out to Hollywood for World Dog Day, though the heat was merciless, so we didn't stay long. The event is to raise awareness and money to stop the killing of dogs for food. It breaks my heart to know this is happening in some countries. I guess that's how some vegans and vegetarians feel about me eating meat, but eating dogs is just inhumane.

22

Oprah and a Chi Tea Latte

I have been having the most curious, recurring dream. I'm at the Starbucks on the Promenade and Oprah walks up beside me. She and I seem to know each other well, as I am not in awe when she appears. Our conversation never changes, which I guess would be the point of a recurring dream.

Oprah: "So, have you tried the chai tea latte?"

Me: "No, I haven't tried it yet."

Oprah: "You should try it. It's really good."

Me: "I'm sure it is, but I'm going to get the vanilla latte."

She smiles at me and says nothing more. And that's it. I have been having this dream for the last couple of months, and lately it occurs more than once a week. I think it's a sign that I too will be a philanthropist like Oprah. I have started the homeless dog campaign and I do have dreams of a no-kill dog shelter that is ran by homeless people. I have this idea that I will have a place for elderly homeless people to live and they will help take care of the dogs. We will do our best to rehabilitate the dogs, and when possible, some of the dogs will become therapy dogs. So, I guess that's what this dream is about since when I Googled, "What does it mean to dream of Oprah," it noted something along the lines of one's nature to be a philanthropist. This excites me, though I am not sure when I will realize this dream. Just knowing it will come to pass brings me immense joy.

23

Not Going Back

I genuinely enjoy my days at Big Brains. The people here are friendly and smart as hell. They've incorporated me into their Big Brain world and it's an honor. I also enjoy having my own office, something I gave up when I moved from Oklahoma and joined the dysfunctional family at Shawshank. I'm sure whatever job I land out here will put me back in a cubicle farm, so I am relishing in this last month of privacy.

I'm going through my emails and there's a name I don't recognize, but the subject sends my heart into palpitations.

From: Jim Rinds

Subject: Welcome to the Team!

I click on the email and glance at the message. It's some dude welcoming me to his team back at Shawshank. I knew my outplacement mentor was working on Plan B just in case I didn't land a position out here, but I never gave it any thought. I can feel the tears welling up in my eyes. I stand to my feet and rush out of my office. Before I know it, I am walking towards the beach.

This email can't be real. He wanted to introduce himself to find out when I would be arriving. I am walking madly to the beach. As I make the two-block walk, tears are engulfing my eyelids. My eyelids can no longer hold the ocean of salty tears, and as I blink, the flood begins.

I keep up my fast and steady pace until I reach the bike trail on the beach. I can barely make out anything around me, as my eyes are drenched with tears. I look behind for the small set of stairs that face the beach. I sit and I cry. I'm wailing. People are walking by, jogging, biking and I'm bawling. There's a homeless man threating to kill all of us sitting on the steps. The sun is beaming down so warmly against my face. But it doesn't comfort me.

I see the homeless man who likes to harass the bikers and runners on the path standing by the bicycle rental hut. I see people enjoying the sand, and others surfing the ocean waves. I see the life I thought I could positively think into being slipping away from me. God, I don't want to go back! Please, God! I promise I will write more – everyday, at least one hour a day. I will stay faithful to this gift you've given me. I will not settle for just living here with a good job but will always work to make writing my full-time career. It will happen. I will not stop until this is my truth, but please, dear God, don't send me back there! It hurts there, it's wrong there. I have no ties to anything there.

The tears won't stop coming and I have no shame in passersby seeing me like this. I'm not even moved by the homeless man threating to kill us.

I must pull myself together and get back to work. Yes, I am ignoring this aching feeling that I will be lonely out here because I know that's just nervousness about being here alone, but I've thought this through. I've moved before to the unknown – like Alabama to Oklahoma and Oklahoma to Virginia. Heck, I've been here a year, so this loneliness crap is crazy. I've made friends here. I have a nice place to live. This is my home now! Besides, I put off doing so much because I thought I wasn't leaving. I didn't make it to Napa Valley, or Santa Barbara, or San Francisco. Are you telling me I've wasted a year and could have done more but didn't? Is this fellowship really coming to an end? I want to start over. Maybe I missed something. I am supposed to be calmer now. I meditate now. I guess I am calmer than I would have been in the past, except the uncontrollable crying. I really thought after last week I was done with that, but I'm not done with tears and seeing this email is making it worse. I DONT WANT TO GO BACK, GOD! WHY IS THIS TURNING OUT TO BE SUCH A HARD THING FOR ME TO ACIVEVE? And why is it every time I think about staying here this overwhelming sense of loneness sweeps over me? What the hell is that?

No, no, no, no, no! God, no! Please, God, no! God, please don't make me go back there, please! I can't. It hurts there. I can't do it. It hurts because it has memories of Dan, it hurts because it's a place I hate, it hurts because I know I've been called to do something better than what awaits me back there. Why can't I stay here and work on that? What is the problem? What am I doing wrong? Am I not faithful enough? Am I not praying enough, not understanding enough? Why is Amy and my new medium, Mona, telling me I'm not going back, but everything is pointing me back? How is it I've put this thought, my desires, out in the universe, but it's not working? Why isn't it working? God, I only want to be here!

Why God? Why? Is it because I'm not writing enough? I know I met with the agent Mickey, and I received wonderful advice at the workshop. I know I'm writing more, but I can do better, I promise. I promise I will write every day to accomplish my dreams. I know I'm writing for the service of others and I'm sorry I've been procrastinating. Oh, God, please let me stay out here. I commit at this very moment to stay true to my craft and I won't slack off anymore, I promise. Am I being punished because I am not working to be a fulltime writer? I just wanted something stable to transition into, God, something to pay the bills, that's why I've applied for all the jobs. Once my writing takes off, I'll quit. I promise. Please don't make me go back there!

My silent pleas to God are shaking me to my core. I am trembling and sobbing. I gain enough focus to see a nice-looking older gentleman smiling at me. He doesn't seem to notice that my face is balled up and saturated with tears. He's just pleasantly smiling and standing next to the homeless man who has since broadened his kill threat to the surrounding area. He doesn't speak, just smiles. I smile back and he walks on.

Seeing him has stopped my tears. I wipe my face and begin to walk towards the beach. I find myself now sitting on the concrete railing. I am still far away from the water, but close enough to hear the waves. I am still, numb. I am just being tested. Yes, that's it. The email is a test of my faith. I still have plenty of applications out there and a month left to find something. It will work out. It will.

I sit a bit longer listening the waves crash against the beach. The sound is forceful and moving. It energizes me and I find the strength to stand. As I head back to work, I take in deep breaths. Walk and breathe, Ava, you've got this. This is where you were meant to be, and no one can take that away from you. God, please forgive me for this moment. I trust you and I know I'm not going anywhere.

24

Inbox

I'm back in my office and back to feeling great. I open my email to respond to Mr. Rinds, but at the top of my inbox is another email. It, too, is from someone I don't know: a Captain Lewis.

From: Capt. Linda Lewis

Subject: Interview for Position AXX6723

Oh, thank you, God! I click on the email and read the message. I've made the cut for a position at Los Angeles Air Force Base! Yep, just a test, Ava, just a test!

I quickly respond to the email requesting I confirm the date and time of the interview. Now, Mr. Rinds, back to you. I find the email from Mr. Rinds and smile. I open it and hit reply.

Mr. Rinds, thank you for such a wonderful welcome to your office. I am not sure if you are aware, but my intentions are to stay on the West Coast, as such I will move forward with all the in-processing paperwork to join your team but please note that should I be selected for a position here, I will remain in the area.

There. Short, sweet, honest. I won't ever meet the man, but I want to be as pleasant about things as possible.

He replies:

Ava,

Yes, your mentor noted your intentions, and I am rooting for your success on the West Coast.

Vr,

Jim Rinds

Done, done, and done! Thank you, God! And thank you for letting me pass this test of faith! I'll have to tell Mona, my medium, about this new development.

Just last night we had a session. It was energy balancing mixed with predictions. I'm not even sure what you call it, but I just know before our session was over, I felt the coolest breeze throughout my body and in the air. This was impressive to me since our session was via the phone.

Mona lives in L.A., but when she offered to have the session via the phone I was intrigued. Energy is energy and it travels, so why not? She said I needed to put fear, worry and doubt aside and be open to all creative ways to stay here. Her insight is spot on and aligns with the Sodalite crystal I purchased last week. The lady at the store said the same thing. I recall she said she heard the Sodalite was the stone I needed. Is that what they call psychic? Anyway, I really enjoy Mona. She too like Amy, Nala, and the lady at the store has this calmness about herself. She is so lighthearted, and our meeting was another one of those Synchrodestiny things. We met at a pet reading for Cleo and Sophie about two months ago. I signed them up thinking it would be fun to get a reading for them, but the session turned out to reveal a lot about me instead.

When we arrived at the pet store, we were escorted to the back where Mona sat in a folding chair. She was looking at her phone when we walk up and when she noticed us, she gave us the grandest smile. Her jet-black curry hair bounced wildly as she stood up to greet us. She was dressed in jeans, a floral blouse, and black flats. She appeared to be about my height and was very slender. She invited me to take a seat across from her and as I did, I felt the strangest feeling -something like a strong breeze wrapping around us.

The session started off a bit odd to me. Cleo and Sophie staring at Mona and Mona staring back at them. Then Mona began to speak and share their thoughts with me. My girls shared their worries for me. They were most worried that I had stopped eating breakfast every morning. I informed Mona that, while oatmeal with blueberries is a nice meal, the cook-to-order chef at Big Brains had won me over with his omelets and French toast. I tried to seem cool and collected about this, but it was blowing my mind. They went on to tell her they didn't like Dan and how excited they were that we no longer spoke. They also informed Mona that they were going to get scrubbed up later that day. When Mona asked what this meant, I said they had a grooming appointment afterwards. Some people don't believe, but I do. This session confirmed my belief. My thought is this – the Bible doesn't say this isn't real, it says stay away from people who use it for evil. Therefore, I embrace it. And Amy also made a connection with the girls. With Amy it was more about how they were feeling and with Mona it was specifics about how I was living my life. Therefore, while both were new experiences for me, our time with Mona took my appreciation of telepathy to a new level.

25

El Segundo

Do people still say "cool as a cucumber" because that's how I'm feeling this morning as I get dressed for this interview. This job is mine and I'm claiming it! I'm dressed in a navy-blue pinstriped suit with matching navy nondescript heels. I'm even wearing pantyhose, something I thought I'd left in the DMV. L.A. is a hosiery-free town. But this is an Air Force interview, so hosiery it is. I got this!

Arriving for my interview, I have not one ounce of nervousness. I make my way upstairs and see a Captain sitting at a desk.

"Good afternoon. You must be Ms. McClure!"

"Good afternoon. Yes, I am."

"Great, take a seat." She points to a chair in front of her desk and smiles. As I do, she stands and walks over to me with a sheet of paper.

"You're right on time, so I can go ahead and give you these."

I take the paper and see they are interview questions: standard procedure for a job with the Air Force. Interview questions are provided fifteen minutes prior to the interview.

I'm reading through the questions and smiling. Easy! I begin to scribble responses, but I feel no sense of worry. These are rookie questions, so I know I got this thing nailed!

As I finish up my notes, I see a woman coming down the hall. She is wearing a sundress and sandals.

"How was it?"

"Not bad. I think I did okay!"

Really? This lady just finished the interview? She's dressed like she's heading to the beach. I know we are in SoCal, but really? I thought Air Force was Air Force everywhere.

My thoughts are disrupted by another lady who appears. She is wearing black slacks, an ocean blue shell, and a white denim jacket.

"Hi. Are you Ava?"

"Yes, hello."

"Hi, I'm Pam. The director. You can come with me."

Wow, okay, she's the boss and she's dressed casually. I'm going to love working here!

Just nailed this interview! I know this job is mine for the following reasons:

1. I gave kick ass answers to every question!
2. After the interview, Pam showed me around the office!
3. The Captain asked me where I would live *once* I got the job, then quickly backpedaled to say *if* I got the job which means she knows they were already eyeing me for the position!
4. As soon as I got in the car, the song "I Left My Wallet in El Segundo" by A Tribe Called Quest was playing on the radio and L.A. Air Force Base is in El Segundo!

Time to find that realtor!

26

Crying on Ventura

It's been over a week, and I am anxiously awaiting an email or phone call about the job. I know it's mine, but it will be nice to get the official confirmation. Today, I've taken the morning off to go to the car dealership and look at some places for rent with a realtor. I'm out in Encino and it's so freaking hot! I've decided to rent before I buy. I want to stay in Santa Monica, but the job is a GS-14 (which is what I currently am) so my salary will not go as far in Santa Monica – but I haven't ruled it out completely. I am also considering Redondo Beach, which is more affordable and closer to the job than any place in the Valley.

I'm driving around the area and I keep looking at the temperature on the dashboard. Man, it's at least 10 degrees hotter out here. I knew this already, as I was out here not long ago when I met Mickey the agent. In either case, I'm open to seeing what I can get out here and who lives in Encino…Shemar Moore, baby!!!

I'm early for my appointment with the realtor, so I drive around to find a parking spot near the first location we will be looking at. After I park, I pick up my phone and check my email. It can't hurt to look. To my surprise, there is an email from the Pam the director. Oh my! How timely is this! Synchrodestiny at its best! I'm house hunting and I get the official notice, what a wonderful testament of faith!

I can feel the big grin on my face as I open the email. My heart is pounding from the excitement. Wait, what, no! I must have misread it. I read the message again. I zero in on the last two sentences:

"We decided to go in a different direction.

I wish you all the best!"

A rejection email? This can't be right. Here come the tears.

This was my last hope. I have to report back to Shawshank in two weeks. My interview was exceptional. I just knew they'd hire me, but instead I receive an email while house hunting in Encino that says I was not selected. I'm so devastated! I start the car and begin to drive down Ventura heading towards Tarzana. I've finally hit a point where I must wipe my tears from my eyes or else risk an accident, as I am blinded from them. I reach for the only napkin I have in the car which had been wrapped around a croissant from earlier this morning. I wipe my eyes and the smell of butter engulfs me. I touch my face and feel the grease. I'm pissed. I'm crying and screaming at the top of my lungs. I am yelling at my Guides, the Angles, and God. I'm having a breakdown on Ventura, and now I'm wiping my face with this greasy ass butter-soaked napkin!

I'm now laughing hysterically. I have to laugh. I have to call the realtor and tell him never mind; I wouldn't be needing a home anywhere on the West Coast. I have to call my Medium. I head back towards Santa Monica. As I do, I'm realizing I would never want to live in The Valley, as it is hot as hell and far away from the beach.

And truthfully, I know in my heart I am not ready to stay here. I was dying to be here, but also dying of the fear of living so far away from everything I know. I felt lonely thinking about it. Sure, this year in SoCal has been great, and yes, this is where I am supposed to be – my allergies cleared up, I commune with an enlightened group of people, my love of writing resurfaced...but I am not one hundred precent ready to be here. I am not ready for the chai tea latte life. That's what Oprah was asking me. Was I ready for change? I clearly knew I was not. I politely said not today and ordered a vanilla latte – the same drink I've order for over a decade. There is something holding me back from genuinely wanting to stay here or maybe something is pulling me back to the DMV or a little bit of both. Maybe there is more for me back East and maybe it has nothing to do with my desire to be here. Maybe the Universe needs me to return -some lessons I've yet to learn, some opportunity that I would miss if I stayed here? I am sad but also okay. If nothing I've learned this year to stay open as I never know what God has for me. And that is the theme of Deepak Chopra's Synchrodestiny course. Okay God. I trust you and I trust me because while I went through all the motions, claimed it to the Universe, applied for over one-hundred jobs, started looking for a new place to live, something in my soul knew the truth and it was my soul who was asking the Universe to please get me back home. And I know I am only able to process this rejection and accept this truth because of all I have gain from this year. Reiki, hypnotherapy, meditation, healing crystals, essential oils sessions and with Mona my medium.

I must return to the Pentagon and the answers will come.

27

Shawshank State of Mind

My medium, Mona, who has evolved into a good friend, said perhaps I am supposed to leave to avoid the big earthquake that is bound to hit the L.A. area in the next couple of years. I said, but what about her and all the others who still live here? She said I couldn't think about that, just this is God's way of keeping me out of harm's way. It has made me feel better, but still, I just want to remain in the area. I was broken open here. I was renewed, reformed even. How can I drive away and return to bureaucratic bullshit?

I am boxing up things to ship back and things to put in the storage unit here and I am emotionally drained. Of everything I ever wanted in my life, this, Lord, was the only one true thing that mattered – at least, so far. My writing is back on, I'm meeting and mixing with people in the industry. I am in my element here. I'm preparing to leave this wonderful world, but I am still at an incredible loss as to why I must leave it. Trust Ava, remember to trust the Universe.

I have been crying every day for weeks. I put on a brave face at work and then I get home, walk the dogs, and breakdown and cry. I don't want to go back to the DMV. I don't know why this is happening, but I trust you, God, and after my breakdown in the car on Ventura Boulevard I should be getting over the idea of staying in Southern California, but I can't. It was all so clear in the moment but as the days pass that understanding that came with the buttery napkin seems to fade away.

I decided to leave a bunch of my things here in storage because I know one of these jobs will eventually come through for me. I am treating this return as an extended business trip. I will go back, I will write this book, and I will use my time back in Shawshank like a journalist on assignment. But I still don't want to go back.

I have been giving great thanks to God for my time here. It occurred to me just the other day that I have been around only white people this year. Sure, there are a few black folks at Big Brains, but I didn't interact with them. Heck I barely interacted with anyone there. I spent the year in my own world out here, wrote a horrible research paper but it was accepted. My crew this year, Tammy, Sarah, Jill, Nala, Mona, Amy back in the DMV – all white. It's been years since this was my reality, since I was living in Oklahoma. As much as I notice race and racism I am surprised I loss that concern for this last year. I am happy I did as all these people plus all those I met in the industry who are also white have been part of my spiritual awakening.

One last trip to the Santa Monica Pier before we head out. We'll be back though. I just know we will. I want to take of picture of us, so I ask two ladies if they would, and they agree. We chat for a while, and they tell me they are Jehovah's Witnesses. One of them goes on to tell me that Jehovah's plan is always correct and that He is having me leave to keep me safe from something out here. Remarkably similar to what Mona said. I do know God will do this, but in my mind, I can't help but wonder why can't He just keep me safe from it without moving me all the way back to the East Coast? I am an hour from hitting the road this morning. I am still not wanting to go.

I met a woman the other day while walking Cleo and Sophie in Palisades Park and curiously her name is Amy. She said she was a psychic and said it had already happened, that I was staying in California yet today I'm loading up the car and starting our first leg of our journey back to Virginia. First stop is Utah. What did she mean it had "already happened"? "It is done," she said. Oh, hell, did I miss something huge? Am I supposed to quit, or defer my retirement? Am I not that big of a risk-taker? No, I'm not. Some of the fellows advised me to start a consulting firm out here, but I don't think I know enough about the DOD to do that. Maybe I have to go back because I didn't take that leap of faith, didn't buy the house like Dan advised. I'm so sorry, God, if I don't trust you enough to leave my job and just live here. But there's a part of me that says I must return to write this book. I need to return for this special assignment as I have started thinking of it, and then I can come back home to Southern California. Maybe that's what she meant. But I still don't want to go. Damn, I thought I'd be full of answers with all my meditating, but they are not coming as fast I would want. I don't know what to do other than to put Cleo and Sophie in this car and leave.

And so, I did; with peace in my heart and awareness that if I remained opened the answers would come, I returned Shawshank. It took a session with Mona and renting a storage unit in Santa Monica where I left most of my things to help me transition back to the DMV. The storage unit is my anchor, my hope and faith that this place is for me someday just not right now.

No Facebook posts on the return trip, just a pocket full of healing crystals. I went out there making all kind of noise, but the return trip was quiet. I didn't have any excitement about returning, just an understanding that I must. I will admit, I did consider turning around the first few days of the trip. I contemplated turning around and going back to L.A. every time I stopped for gas. What if I went rogue and just didn't come back – quit and never looked back? But I needed to be sensible, right?

Plus, there's Sally. She showed up two nights before I left California. I was lying on my bed after taking one of my super-hot baths and I saw her in my peripheral vision. She was dressed in a white dress with a scarf tied around her head. This should have shocked the shit out of me but instead I was unbothered. After about five minutes she faded away. I didn't immediately know who she was, but I was fairly certain. The next day I looked up Sally Hemings and I knew it was she who had visited me the night before. I am not sure what she wants but she appeared again in my hotel room in Pittsburgh. I was eating my dinner and there she was again standing beside me. I didn't look directly at her, but I knew it was the same person, or should I saw ghost or spirt or soul.

I understand that I must take a trip to Monticello, Thomas Jefferson's home, Sally's home – another reason to return to the East Coast. I am intrigued. I've never had a ghost or spirt or soul or whatever it was come to visit me in my waking state. There's been my grandmother but only in my dreams.

I must admit California brought many things into my life -Reiki, meditation, crystals, essential oils, a friend who's a Medium, meeting a psychic in the park and now the spirit of a famous slave. It is certainly a fascinating way to wrap up this year!

* * *

Meeting Mr. Sexy at the Kennedy Center

I'm dressed in my cobalt blue summer dress though it is December and freaking freezing here in Arlington. I am headed to the Kennedy Center. I purchased a ticket to see the one, the only, the immaculate Diana Ross! I have been in love with her since I was a little girl. There is something about her grace, her elegance, her charm, and her ability to seemingly float across the stage that has always captivated me.

While I have seen Ms. Ross before, this is a special treat for me because she appeared in my dream and told me everything I wanted would happen in the next one to two years. I'm excited about that because maybe it means not only I'm heading back to California but in the next year or two my novel about Shawshank will be a number one best seller and a blockbuster movie!

As I pull up to the Kennedy Center fond memories drift into my thoughts. My friends and I have spent many nights here enjoying performances from the Alvin Ailey Dance Theater to the Nutcracker ballet. I recall coming here one night and eating across the street at The Watergate Hotel many years ago with my friends. It was an interesting place, and we were the only brown spots in the restaurant. Rich older white people come to The Watergate Hotel for dinner is what I gathered after looking around, but it didn't matter as it was my first time at the Kennedy Center to see The Nutcracker ironically during this exact time in December, but the year was 2008.

Here I am now eight years later rolling solo. I didn't invite any of my friends because I know them, they're slow and they are always on CP (colored people's) time, and I would have been frustrated. Plus, there was only one seat remaining in the orchestra section and I want to be as close to Ms. Ross as possible therefore I'm here alone.

As I exit my car and head up to Will Call. I'm feeling quite fabulous and sexy. This dress is turning heads not to mention I've got crochet braids in my hair which are giving me long curly locks hitting my waist.

I swing by to pick up my ticket from Will Call. I'm here early so there's no rush just me and time.

Out of the corner of my eye I see a man and I feel the need to turn to take a look. He is quite handsome. Tall, blonde, and chiseled. He is wearing a black suit, with a slender gray tie. I smile in delight of his presence, and he smiles back. If feels like we're smiling and staring at each other for hours. I notice the person in front of me move. I shake my head and move to the next window.

"Hello ma'am. May I help you?"

"Yes, thank you. Ava McClure.

"Here's your ticket. Enjoy the show."

"Thank you very much!"

I am beaming on the inside! I can't believe I'm going to see Diana Ross perform with the National Symphony Orchestra! Her voice with an orchestra, what more could anyone ask for?

As I exit Will Call there he is again walking by only this time as he passes we are only about two feet apart. He turns, stops, and stares at me and I feel a rush of energy as if there's this force flowing between his body and mine. I'm drawn to him. It is magnetizing.

"Hello. I must say that you are the most beautiful woman I've ever seen!"

"Thank you."

I think I am smiling but I might be standing here with my mouth wide open and gawking.

"My name is Lucas."

Do I detect an accent?

"Hi, I'm Ava."

"What brings you here tonight?"

"I'm here to see Diana Ross."

"Ah that's wonderful! Yes, I'm here to meet a business partner and his wife. There is a ballet in the Opera House tonight."

"Yes I heard about that but between Diana Ross and the ballet I had to choose Diana Ross."

Lucas laughs, "I don't blame you! I would have chosen Diana Ross too, but this is a business thing."

"Of course."

I smile back. I can't take my eyes off of this man. His piercing blue eyes are rather hypnotizing.

"Would it be OK if I gave you my number?"

I'm remembering the movie *He's Just Not That Into You*. What's the rule? If he gives you his number, he's not that into you?

"You can but I could give you my number."

I think this is how it's supposed to go. I am having a hard time remembering the movie right now.

"Oh, of course I didn't want seem too forward, but I will certainly take your number!"

He hands me his phone and I put in my number. I hand it back and he smiles.

"Ava, enjoy your night! I hope you have a wonderful evening!"

"You too Lucas! It was nice meeting you!"

We part ways and I turn to head to the Concert Hall. The doors haven't opened yet and the line is wrapped around the corner but it's a fun experience as I am chatting with an older couple in front of me though I must admit these Ivanka Trump shoes I'm wearing while cute as heck are taking my feet to new levels of pain. But I've got to hand it to her she managed to make the perfect nude color heel that matches my complexion perfectly!

As the doors open and the crowd begins to move forward, I see my phone light up in my purse I pull it out and see it is a text from Lucas:

It was really nice meeting you just now Ava. I look forward to speaking with you tomorrow.

I reply:

It was nice meeting you too. I am looking forward to chatting as well.

Well, Lucas must be into me! We'll see how things go tomorrow. I am looking forward to our chat. Returning to the DMV and being free and clear of Dan has made for a nice transition back. Maybe Lucas is the reason I'm back and my investigative journalism of Shawshank for my novel of course.

Meeting a sexy Latino man at the Kennedy Center and I've only been back a couple of months, I think that's a pretty nice start to life back on the East Coast!

My Dysfunctional Love Affair with the Pentagon

My time is ending at Shawshank. The place I cried about returning to is now the place I'm sad to leave. My new job is out of the building, and I'm being paroled again. Only this time not to sunny Santa Monica but dreary Maryland. In either case I'm being released. I should feel elated about this but somehow Shawshank has become my home again. I fought like crazy not to return from California and now just one year back in this place I my heart sinks a little at the thought of saying goodbye. Most of my friends are here, plus the familiar faces of people I've seen for years in the halls and at the various locations. I never bothered to know most of their names, but we know each other just the same. The water delivery guy, the custodians, the folks that work at Burger King and Subway. I'm sad to be leaving. Scared about what lies ahead for the new job? No. I know God has me fully equipped for whatever they have in store for me. I'm not sad to move on to the new job but sad to leave this place. Sad to leave this office where just the other day I asked a co-worker who was stressing out if she'd ever tried alternate nostril breathing. She and another co-worker busted into laughter, and I replied - oops I went too Zen on you it's now my home. But they too will move on, the military will PCS (Permenant Change of Station) the civilians will find another office to serve time in and the faces in this space will change. But the culture will not. The DoDism will remain. The Groundhog Dayness will be here always. It's rather comforting. I have been institutionalized - a little bit yet I'm clear on my escape and I chip away daily, like Andy, only I do it by writing. I wrote what the Hollywood executives told me to write. I'm now editing the great piece of work and I am going to have to keep expanding my vibrations to not allow myself to get sucked up in this place. To not look up and have done another twenty years here in the Pentagon.

I'm saddened. I'm almost numb I'm so at peace but aware that leaving this place is a separation from my home my Pentagon family.

Today I don't see Shawshank. I see people who get it the Groundhog Dayness that is. People who are not taking their yard break but rest before the next round of crazy. They don't explode with anger they are just being. I bet these are the ones who have magnificent work life balance. I've been seeing them wrong all this time and now I am them one week before I leave one week before the unknown but it's the only way to continue to grow. Maybe they are disgruntled heck I don't know their stories but today I choose to see them this way.

Today I see my life and where a lot of changes and growth occurred. I look over this courtyard and see where Dan and I met. I see unhappy unfulfilled Ava who was not yet awakened, not enlightened.

I think though my sadness is more about change. It's not the new location of the job but knowing with every fiber of my being that I will never work in this building again – that this new position in Maryland is my final stopping point on this DoD train. I will complete this clever work of literature and it will free me from my servitude altogether. This is not vanity but actuality. It's as clear as I am a human. As steady as my faith in God.

I am wrapping up this book at the same time I am wrapping up my time at Shawshank. There's meaning to this. Much like my Oprah dreams. They didn't stop after my Venture cry fest last year, but they have changed slightly. We are always in a Starbucks and she's asking me if I've tried the chai tea latte and I say yes, She goes on to say how happy she is that it's doing well for me. I see more to this dream now that I say yes to the chai tea latte. I see it from her beginnings and where she is now. I see her not sticking to the safe way but making a way. I see her believing in herself and living her life's purpose. She could still be a local TV news personality but instead she is known around the world and that is my destiny as well. The safe way is no longer my path. I will move to this new position and stay for just a few months and then draft my freedom papers (my letter of resignation) and live out my soul's purpose!

ERICKA "TARA" REYNOLDS

Mindfulness Life Coach | Spiritual Counselor | Reiki Master |
Chopra Health Instructor | Sound Healer | Hypnotist

www.taradevima.com

Services I Provide to Support You and Your Animals:

Soul Invigoration Sessions

The Soul Invigoration Experience is for those who desperately want to change but are holding themselves back.

This was me a few years ago. I was miserable and finding no satisfaction in my personal life and career. BUT.. after I channeled a beautiful healing practice and began to incorporate it into my daily life I gained the self-love, strength and faith to walk away from my six-figure high profile career at the Pentagon and live out my soul's mission!

I fully support you *BREAKING THE CHAINS* of a self-enslaved life with the powerful scientifically proven practices of Ayurveda and beautiful alternative healing modalities!

Break the chains of whatever you have enslaved yourself in that does not serve you.. your job, your romantic relationship, your family, friends, yourself. and rediscover your SOUL!

A Soul Invigoration Experience will assist you in tapping into your essence, your soul, your innermost most knowing. It will *awaken you* from the daily drudge and toll you feel and lift you to your highest self!

I am living proof of my method and I know how to fully support you on your journey I even wrote a novel series about it!

Our time together is a **safe sacred space**where we discuss you and your life. We tap into the unspoken desires of your heart and allow your soul to appear. I use my *psychic and medium abilities* to support the reconnection with your soul so you can discover your soul's purpose abundantly and limitless!

Experiences are offered virtually as 16-week sacred containers of time to fully assist your transformation and may be purchased in full or as a scription with four payment installments.

After our 16 weeks together, you can connect with me as needed with 90-minute Soul Invigoration Sessions.

** Individual 90 minutes sessions are also available for those seeking to add a boost to their current mindfulness practice!**

I use several healing aids in addition to Reiki to support you, to awaken your senses, to assist in manifesting your soul's desire.

A session includes:
- Energy Healing (Always Included)
- Customized Hypnotic Track (Always included)
- Ayurveda Teachings
- Sound Healing
- Intuitive Counseling
- Breathwork
- Guided Meditation
- Crystal Healing

- Essential Oils
- Affirmations
- Visualization Exercises
- Chakra Balancing
- Mudras
- Mantras
- Motion and Flow Exercises
- Card Readings

Energy Healing/Reiki is the transference of life force energy which allows for relaxation and restoration of the mind body and soul the clearing of auras and Chakra balancing. I conduct Reiki for to you discover your essential self to allow life force energy to flow through me as a vessel for the relaxation and healing of your mind body and soul, to invigorate you to find and live out your life's purpose so you may live a glorious life and be a blessing to others!

Ayurveda Teachings provide education from the ancient 5000 year old Indian healing system and covers areas such as nutrition, sleep and emotional well-being.

Sound Healing with singing bowls is used to support relaxation and aids in reduction of stress and anxiety. It is also supportive of the immune system, pain relief and mental and emotional focus.

Intuitive Counseling is the ability for one to serve as the vessel for messages given by spirit guides. I conduct my sessions with the love and support of a beautiful spirit team. As such I am gifted with the ability to provide you with keen insight and answers to questions through my spirit guides.

Breathwork is the conscious focus on breath to invoke a sense of calm and relaxation. I use breathwork to assist you in dropping into the moment, to become fully present and relaxed so you are able get the most out of your session.

Guided Meditation uses narration to assist in the relaxation of the mind body and soul. You are guided to a scene that invokes calm and tranquility. I use this form of meditation to induce relaxation and allow you to fully embrace the Reiki session.

Crystal Healing crystals are a part of Mother Earth's healing energy and are a source of healing and protection. I use crystals in my sessions to address your specific areas of concern and compliment the healing energy from the Reiki.

Essential Oils are derived from Mother Earth and support the healing of the mind body and soul. I use essential oils as aromatherapy to support you with your specific areas of concern and compliment the healing energy from the Reiki.

Affirmations are a beautiful way to gently recondition the mind. I provide you with channeled affirmations I receive from my spirit team.

Visualization Exercises are powerful tools use to support manifestation of desired future events. I use this technique at the end of the Reiki session to gently guide you into a loving peaceful place in the future where you experience living the life you desire.

Charka Balancing/Healing helps bring the mind, body and soul into harmony and flow.

Mudras are hand gestures used to support healing and relaxation.

Mantras are sounds which are repeated and support the calming of the nervous system and building confidence and internal strength.

Motion and Flow uses a variety of yoga poses to support mind, body soul alignment.

Oracle Card Readings are used to provide guidance and insight into one's life and spiritual journey. I use the cards to help guide our conversation and to assist the you in expressing what is resonating in your heart. Card reading is a gentle way to provide you with answers to support your spiritual journey.

Distance Sessions

Energy knows love and is boundless. It travels through space and time to send healing for the mind, body and soul.

Distance healing is a beautiful way to honor yourself - to give yourself the love and healing it deserves. When the mind, body and soul is at peace, healing and enlightenment can take place.

A distance healing session is quite similar to an in person and includes connecting via Zoom and the oils and crystals are used on me with the intention placed for you. While we are not in the same room I still serve as the vessel and channel beautiful loving healing energy to you.

Hypnosis Support with Hypnotic Tracks

It is my desire to support you in manifesting your heart's desires!

Together we work to understand you, your goals, and limiting beliefs. With this information I create a customized hypnotic track for you!

We will spend 90 minutes together which includes guided breathwork and meditation exercises. Mindfulness is the foundation to manifestation and these exercises will allow you to start to build upon your daily practice.

90 Minute Virtual Consultation

Consultation Details:

- Breathwork and Mediation exercises with instructions for performing on your own
- Relaxation Tips handout
- Personalize affirmations to support you while awaiting the delivery of your hypnotic track.
- Hypnotic Track. Tracks are delivered as MP4 files within 10 days of your consultation and should be listened to daily for 21 days. It is a small commitment to achieve enormous results!
- Customized waken state affirmation track (for those who complete end of 21 day survey)

Animal Healology (founded by Ericka 'Tara" Reynolds)

The integration of animals and their parents, mindfulness practices, Reiki and many other healing modalities to support the health and well-belling of our animals!

I serve as a Soul Invigoration Guide using the practice of Reiki, along with essential oils, healing crystals and channel counseling to assist in the healing of physical, emotional and behavior issues. I believe the wellbeing of animals is directly linked to the wellness of their parents therefore my sessions include time connecting with the animal as well as animal and parent bonding time through breathwork, affirmations and meditation. My sessions are designed to promote healing and relaxation for the soul, body and mind. It's A Family Affair!

Animal parents also receive a copy of helpful human relaxation tips to assist with ultimate soul invigoration for the entire family.

I also provide Natural Animal Remedies Workshops where I provide animal parents with education and guidance on a variety of topics to include energy healing, essential oils, crystals, earthing, and flower remedies.

Spiritual Cleansing

My cleansing ceremonies are customized to support you and your needs and includes a Reiki healing for you as well. A typical ceremony will have the following elements:

- A special house/office gift cleansed and charged with Reiki for you
- A customized essential oil blend
- Grounding and centering of those present for the ceremony
- Cleansing Ceremony - Clearing of negative energy and brining in good positive supportive energy with smudging, sound healing, crystals or outdoor activities (customized to support your needs and any special considerations such as animals in the home)
- Reiki healing for you and all those present for the ceremony
- A dedication of love and positive energy to include stated intentions for you and those participating in the ceremony

Teaching and Education

A large part of my soul's mission is to educate others!

Throughout the year I offer a variety of classes! These classes are ideal for supporting your spiritual growth and wellness and for those seeking to be of service to others! Classes include:

- Reiki Level I, II, III and Reiki Master Teacher Certifications
- Animal Healology Certification
- Ayurvedic Health Classes
- Beginning Your Mindfulness Practice Workshops
- Building Your Wellness Toolkit Workshops
- Essential Oils for People Workshops
- Animal Alternative Healing Modalities Workshops
- Essentials for Animals Workshops

Speaking Engagements

Sharing my story is part of my mission to educate, inspire and entertain. I am always happy to support events that serve to uplift others!

Credentials

Mindfulness Life Coach, April 2022

Ayurvedic Lifestyle Teacher, Chopra Education, May 2021

Hypnotist , Granja Vortex Method, January 2021

Sound Healer, September 2020 Reiki Master, July 2020

Lightworker and Inner Harmony, November 2017

Accreditations

Mindfulness Life Coach, To be completed by September 2021
Aromatherapy, Complementary Therapists Accredited Association,
     May 2020
Spirituality Coach, Complementary Therapists Accredited
     Association, May 2020

Training

Energy Flow (Breathwork, Tibetan Breath Yoga and Pranayama,
     meditation, mindfulness and relaxation techniques)
Canine Acupressure, January 2021
Healing Flower Essences and Crystals for Animals, December 2020
Animal Communication, December 2019
Natural Pet Remedies, June 2018

Education

MBA, Oklahoma City University, August 1998
BS, Accounting, Alabama State University, May 1995